CAREERS IN TELEVIS
by Jeanne Nagle

CAREERS IN WEB DESIGN* W
by Walter Oleksy   AD438   ©2001

CAREERS IN THE MOVIES*
by Marlys H. Johnson   AD438   ©2001

FALL 2001

CAREERS AS A PROFESSIONAL PHOTOGRAPHER
by Greg Roza   ©2001

CAREERS IN ANIMAL CARE AND VETERINARY SCIENCE* ✓
by Deborah A. Marinelli   AD438   ©2001

CAREERS IN COMPUTER ANIMATION ✓
by Jeremy Shires   ©2001

CAREERS IN MODELING
by Kerri O'Donnell   ©2001

CAREERS IN PHYSICAL THERAPY ✓
by Trisha Hawkins   ©2001

SPRING 2002

CAREERS IN OUTER SPACE: New Business Opportunities
by Edward Willett   ©2002

CAREERS IN SPORTS MEDICINE B
by Barbara Moe   ✓ ©2002

FALL 2002

CAREERS IN VIDEO AND DIGITAL VIDEO* ✓
by Paul Allman   AD012   Rev. ©2001
                    NCAN4960-720809-AR8.1-10.3

MAY BE PURCHASED INDIVIDUALLY $19.95

THE CAREER RESOURCE LIBRARY

Careers
in
WEB DESIGN

Walter Oleksy

The Rosen Publishing Group, Inc.
New York

To Justin and Kaitlyn Lee Ohde, young Web surfers

Published in 2001 by The Rosen Publishing Group, Inc.
29 East 21st Street, New York, NY 10010

Copyright © 2001 by Walter Oleksy

First Edition

All rights reserved. No part of this book may be reproduced in any form without permission in writing from the publisher, except by a reviewer.

Library of Congress Cataloging-in-Publication Data

Oleksy, Walter G., 1930–
Careers in Web design / by Walter Oleksy — 1st ed.
   p. cm.
ISBN 0-8239-3191-9
   1. Web sites—Design—Vocational guidance. [I. Title. II. Series.]
TK5105.888 .O42296 2000
005.7'2—dc21   00-010323

Manufactured in the United States of America

About the Author

Walter Oleksy received a bachelor of arts degree in journalism from Michigan State University. He has worked as a writer and editor for over thirty years.

He was a feature writer for the *Chicago Tribune* and editor of two national magazines before writing over thirty books for adults, teenagers, and preteens. He has also written numerous articles, many of them on computer-related subjects, that have appeared in national magazines.

Oleksy's other books on computer technology for Rosen include *Web Entrepreneur* and *Video Game Designer*. He also authored a four-book series, *The Information Revolution*, describing the uses of computer and audio-video technology in science, education, industry, and entertainment.

For a complete list of Oleksy's books, go to: *http://home.earthlink.net/~waltmax/bio.html*

Acknowledgments

The author wishes to thank members of the International Webmasters Association, the HTML Writers Guild, and the World Organization of Webmasters for their help in writing this book.

Contents

Introduction	1

SECTION I: The World of the Web

1. The Career of a Web Designer/Developer	10
2. Preparing for Your Web Career	19
3. Learn Web Design in High School	40

SECTION II: Working as a Web Designer

4. Getting Your First Job	56
5. Meet Web Designers/Developers	66
6. The Making of a Web Site	87
7. Looking to the Future	113
Glossary	125
For More Information	128
For Further Reading	131
Index	133

Introduction

Few things move more swiftly or change faster than the worlds of computers and information technology. About ten years ago, few people outside the computer industry knew the Internet existed. Today, with an estimated one billion Web pages on-line throughout the world, the Web is considered to be the fastest growing part of the Internet, and those who know how to design, develop, and maintain Web sites are among the most sought-after in the information technology industry.

The Internet is a computer network. It connects millions of computers all over the world to send and receive information and graphics. The World Wide Web is a set of software on the Internet, called "the Web" for short, that supports text, graphics, music, and movies. That software is a set of programs that tell a computer what to do.

A Web page or Web site is a place computer users go on the Internet to get information, conduct business, play games, and do a million other things. Web pages not only revolutionized how we conduct business and gather or exchange information, they created a new major career within the world of computers.

Creating Web sites requires the skills of both a Web designer and a Web developer. Sometimes, one person does both jobs, but more often they are done by two or more people. Web designers focus on the actual look and feel of the Web site. They create the text and graphics that make up a Web page. They work with Web developers who take the graphics that the designer makes and then generate the site with the necessary scripting or programming.

"Jobs in computer fields top the list of occupations that will see the fastest growth and greatest demand for workers through at least the year 2006," says a spokesperson for the U.S. Bureau of Labor Statistics. Web designers and developers earn $30,000 or more in entry-level positions, and salaries for those with two years of experience average $61,600.

Each day, more businesses, institutions, and individuals are hiring people with Web design skills to create a presence for them on the Internet. These Web sites give out information, advertise, and sell products or services. Industry forecasters predict Web designers will continue to be in demand far into the future.

This book will tell you about the exciting world of the Web and the career of creating Web sites. You will learn how and why careers in Web design and development are important, promising, and pay well. Next, you will learn how to prepare for such careers, even while you are in high school.

One of the best ways to learn about any career is to meet people working in that field. In subsequent chapters you will meet young men and women who describe their work as salaried Web designers and developers for corporations that sell products or services, and also people who work for companies whose business it is to create Web sites for those corporations. You will also meet others who work for themselves as freelance Web designers and developers. They tell how they trained for their jobs, what they do, how they do it, what they earn, and what they like or dislike about their work. They also offer advice on how you can get started in this exciting and rewarding career.

In a separate section of the book, you will learn how Web sites are designed and developed. Finally, you will find a list of organizations, individuals, and on-line sources that offer a wealth of information and tips on creating Web sites and learning more about careers in this field of computer technology.

Technology of the Web

The Web connects servers to the Internet and provides an easily used and understood method of accessing electronic content. Accessing information requires communication between a browser client and a server application.

Browsers, such as Netscape, Internet Explorer, and Mosaic, are software applications used to surf the Web. A Web server is a networked host computer that contains files of text, graphics, and sound that are served to clients by way of HTML. HTML stands for hypertext markup language, which is a computer code, or language, used to create hypertext. Hypertext is a code that "speaks" to computers and tells them what to do. HTML commands tell your browser how to display each page, which typeface or font to use, which graphics to display, and how to link to other documents.

To see what HTML code looks like, go to a Web page and click the "Source" or "View Document Source" command under the "View" menu in your browser. You will see that HTML code is like a computer-language version of shorthand, with symbols that stand for instructions instead of words.

Accessing content (text, graphics, sound, etc.) through the Web consists of communication between a browser client and the server utilizing HTTP. HTTP stands for hypertext transfer protocol, the system of delivering HTML documents from the Web to the user's computer. Hypertext links enable users to move from one document on the Web to another. Links are connections between Web page documents.

Internet Terms

In computer terminology, a page on the World Wide Web is another word for a document object. An object on the Web is a piece of data in the form of a file. On-line, a Web page is a single page that is one continuous piece of data. A Web site is a set of related interlinked pages. A link on a Web page enables viewers to move to other parts of the page where related information or graphics can be found.

The Internet enables people all over the globe to communicate in ways even more revolutionary than the telephone and telegraph. This is because computer and Internet technology provide what has been called an electronic "information highway."

Web sites have become a new and productive means of electronically buying and selling, revolutionizing the

Introduction

worlds of advertising, marketing, and commerce. Perhaps their greatest benefit is that they allow people to communicate with others in a way hardly dreamed of just a decade ago.

History of the Web

The World Wide Web could not have been created without the computer. In turn, the computer owes its origin to the first modern calculating machine invented by the French philosopher and mathematician Blaise Pascal (1623-1662). Its evolution into today's modern computers took years.

The first real digital computer was designed by an Englishman, Charles Babbage (1791-1871), and his associate, Ada Lovelace (1815-1852), after whom the programming language Ada was named. The need for faster calculating of the national census in America in 1890 led a young army engineer and statistician, Hermann Hollerith (1860-1929), to invent a tabulating device involving use of punched cards to store information.

The first fully electronic calculating machine, the ENIAC (the Electronic Numerical Integrator and Computer), was created by American scientists to help the Allies in World War II. It was developed during the 1940s by J. Presper Eckert and John W. Mauchly at the University of Pennsylvania's Moore School of Electrical Engineering. The thirty-ton computer, containing vacuum tubes, wiring, and other components, enabled scientists and the military to calculate mathematical equations required to accurately aim ballistic missiles.

The invention of the transistor by a team of Nobel Prize-wining physicists at the Bell Telephone Laboratories in 1948 enabled computers to become faster and smaller. Integrated circuitry in the 1950s further advanced computer technology, which led to the creation of "supercomputers" that perform millions of operations per second. Improvements in computer technology resulted in today's desktop and laptop computers that can operate thousands of times more efficiently than the creators of the thirty-ton ENIAC ever dreamed.

Evolution of the Web

The Web began as a system with text and no graphics. It has evolved into a multimedia adventure that can include video, animation, and sound. The Internet goes back to 1945, when Vannevar Bush published *As We May Think*, describing a microfilm-based device he called the "memex" in which a person stored books, records, and communications. It was mechanized so that it could be consulted fast and flexibly, and more could be added by "scanning" documents into the device. A memex operator could create what Bush called "trails," where documents and notes were linked together into a personalized information system. Today Bush's "trails" are called "links."

In 1965, Ted Nelson wrote about his version of a future worldwide information and communication network in a book called *Literary Machines*. He called his brainchild Project Xanadu and wrote about "hypertext" and "hypermedia." Xanadu (ZA-na-doo) would be "a unifying system of order for all information including electronic publishing, personal work, organization of files, and corporate work." It also allowed documents to be linked.

The Web as it is known today began in 1989. Tim Berners-Lee and Robert Cailliau created the concept of hypertext-based systems for the purpose of sharing documentation and high energy physics (HEP) documents. A year later, they created software to accomplish this and called the system the World Wide Web.

The Web began to spread in the high-energy physics community. Stanford University set up the first Web server in the United States, called the Stanford Linear Accelerator Center. By the end of 1992, there were fifty Web servers in the world.

History of Web Design

The first Web designers and developers were literate in computer and information technology—many were physicists who worked with Internet-connected workstations in their offices or laboratories. The first generation of graphical browsers, such as Mosaic, Viola, and Midas, were introduced in 1993. They opened the Web to more people, and by the year's end, 200 more Web servers had been added. Webmasters who knew HTML, the language of Web design, were both the designers and information architects who created early Web sites.

Articles about the new technology began appearing in magazines and newspapers, which spread the word about the Internet. By the end of 1994, there were 2,500 Web servers worldwide that were using new software for most operating systems, including Unix, VM/CMS, VMS, Microsoft Windows, MS-DOS, and MacOS.

As the Web became more widely used, it became clear that the work of creating Web sites required the skills of more than just one person. Thus began the concept of a team of workers to put together Web sites, and a Webmaster—who formerly did it all alone—to oversee the entire process. The Web design team included graphic designers, programmers, and information architects.

Careers in Web Design

Since these beginnings—only a few short years ago—the billion Web sites already on-line forecast a future in which a majority of the people of the world operate computers and surf the Web. As Pal Saffo, a computer industry consultant at the Institute of the Future in Menlo Park, California, puts it: "It's pretty easy to imagine that in a fairly short period of time—say within ten years—to be a member of society and not be on-line and surfing Web pages will be like living in Los Angeles and not having a car."

Someone will have to create those Web sites for which businesses spend some $19 billion each year. They may earn $25,000 a year to start, and with a few years' experience become Webmasters earning upward of $100,000. Will one of tomorrow's Web designers be you?

The next chapter will give you a brief overview of the work involved in designing Web sites. Whether one person or a team of people design the sites, the skills and tasks required are varied, mainly involving knowledge of computers, writing, graphics, and design.

Section I
The World of the Web

The Career of a Web Designer/Developer

Web designers and/or developers perform the basic job of creating, implementing, and maintaining sites on the Web. Although the term "Web page" can be used to describe a site on the Internet, it is misleading because most Web sites are more than just one page on a computer monitor. While a simple Web page may consist of text and graphics on a specific subject, more complex sites are often a series of pages with links to pages with more specific information. They may also link to other Web sites. More sophisticated Web pages may use "frames" (areas of the page that can be scrolled), animation, and sound. They may also contain "applets" (options that the viewer can download for interactive information).

There are often two distinct types of jobs involved in creating a Web site: the Web designer and the Web developer. Sometimes, one person has the skills necessary to perform both tasks. However, in creating more complex

Web developers create, implement, and maintain Web sites.

sites, such as those involving interactive features, each job may be the responsibility of a separate person with specialized skills.

Web designers are in charge of establishing the visual experience of a site. They create or oversee the creation of graphics, choose and sometimes manipulate photographs for the site, and define the interactive experience for the site. Primarily, a Web designer will have a strong creative and artistic background, but must also have a working understanding of HTML (hypertext markup language, the most popular Internet programming language), JavaScript and Flash (languages which add animation), and other Web technologies.

Web developers are in charge of creating the functionality of a site. Typically, they will put together the code that defines a user's experience of the site. A good Web developer is able to turn a Web site into a functional and vital tool for business and commerce. Web designers often collaborate with Web developers in the creation of a Web site. Their work may be overseen by Webmasters who are expert Web designers and/or developers. In this book, you will learn about the work of both Web designers and Web developers—who are often collectively known as Web creators—as well as learning about the skills and duties of Webmasters.

Web Skills

Those who create Web pages must have a general knowledge of computers, know how to network (communicate with other professionals), and have writing, graphic, business, and marketing skills. One person may do all the work in designing a simple Web site, but a team of specialists, each person having at least one of those skills, is often required to create more complex sites.

Web designers and developers often work together to plan the look and content of a Web site, and a Webmaster may oversee their plan. Then the designer begins the work necessary to implement those plans.

Designers work for a wide variety of commercial users, ranging from giant corporations to small businesses, as well as for organizations, government agencies, educational institutions, and individuals who want to tell the world about themselves.

The need for Web designers in business and industry is so great that IBM began recruiting more than 100 Web designers as part of its Web Integrator Initiative just as this book was being written. According to Tim Scannell of Enterprise Partner, who tracks careers in the information technology field, nearly every major firm is looking for qualified Web designers.

Salary Versus Freelance

A Salaried Web Designer/Developer

There are basically two types of Web designers/developers: those who work for a company and those who are self-employed. Salaried Web designers and developers earn from $35,000 to $50,000 a year. Those who are self-employed may earn more or less, depending on the number of Web sites they work on. Many Web designers/developers work for a business or organization and are on a regular salary to create its official presence on the Web. They work in-house at the business or organization's office on a daily basis. Some examples of this type of worker include:

— Those who work for a major automobile manufacturing company, creating a site that describes the company's new line of cars and trucks.
— Those who work for a bank, designing its site so that those with savings or checking accounts can get account information, transfer funds, and do other business with the bank by computer rather than in-person.
— Those who work for a university, creating a site that both promotes the university and sends out information about its academic programs.

- Those who work for an organization that monitors medical researchers and their clinical testing. The Web designer creates an Internet site that describes the organization's efforts.
- Those who work for a design house—a firm whose business is to produce Web sites for clients such as businesses and organizations. Design and maintenance of a Web site can be less expensive for a business or organization if it hires the services of a company specializing in creating Web sites.

The Web designer/developer at a design house may work at the client company (considered a secondary employer) only part of the time, learning what the client's needs are. Then the designer/developer may return to his or her computer at the office of the design firm (the primary employer) to actually create the site for the client company.

A Freelance Web Designer/Developer

Many other Web designers do not work as salaried employees for a business or organization, or for a firm that creates Web sites. They are self-employed, or freelance, Web designers. They have the same skills and do the same work as their salaried peers but are paid on a per-job basis. They often work from home, driving to the offices of clients to learn their Web site needs, then returning to their home computers to create the site.

An example of a freelance Web designer is Jimmy Turner, who worked for a magazine publishing company, designing its Web site. After a few years, he decided he preferred being self-employed, so he found clients who needed his skills. His first client was a building contractor who hired him to create a Web site that described the new homes he and his crew built.

Another example is Irene Kennedy, who became a freelance Web designer right after graduating from college with a degree in computer science. She designed the Web site for a small chain of video rental stores. A salaried Web designer working full-time at the chain's main store would be too expensive, so a freelance designer was sought. Ms. Kennedy was hired on a per-job basis to design the chain's Web site and to maintain it. That requires her to upgrade it each month with information and graphics about new movies released on video and DVD.

Intranet and Extranet Web Pages

On the Web, there are both intranet sites and extranet sites, both requiring skilled designers. Intranet sites are accessible only to those working for a company on its internal network. This private system enables employees in different offices or departments to communicate with each other to perform their work more efficiently. It also allows employers to communicate information more effectively to their employees regarding corporate news or things like changes in insurance and other benefit programs. Extranet sites are secured connections where special users such as customers can enter a special, secured area on the Internet where they can conduct business. The sites are often used to place orders and exchange corporate information a company wishes to be private rather than public.

There are many professional opportunities available for women in the field of Web design.

Occupational Outlook

An estimated eight million Web designers will be needed to fill jobs in this growing field at least through the year 2006, according to the World Organization of Webmasters. Most, or 86 percent of the required number of designers, will be full-time employees creating Web sites for a primary employer. The rest will be freelancers designing on a per-job basis.

Web design is considered an excellent choice of work for young people who like working with computers and the Internet. Some 35 percent of those employed as Web designers in 2000 were between the ages of twenty-five and thirty-five. Most of them, or 72 percent, were in their first Web design position, according to the industry publication, *Web Week*. These figures are proof that clients in need of Web designers look to young people who are computer literate, with skills they learned in high school and/or college.

Find Web Jobs on the Internet

You can get an idea of the number of positions available for Web designers by doing a general on-line search on a career site, such as Monster.com. You will find help wanted notices such as the following:

Web Designer
Needed: Someone who can design Web page from scratch. Bachelor of science degree or experience equivalent in HTML, Java, and other design languages.

Web Designer/Team Leader
Billion-dollar information services consulting firm seeks technical professional. Must possess five years' experience; know Visual Basic, HTML, JavaScript. Good communication skills and the ability to be a team leader.

Web Developer
Developer needed for Stamps.com, a site that sells commemorative postage stamps to collectors. Previous Web page programming a must; knowledge of page generation to e-commerce.

Temporary Web Designer
Looking for someone to help develop a Web site for a telecommunications company. Work will take about one week. HTML knowledge required.

Web Designer
Hiring full-time designer for rock concert promoting company. Please respond via e-mail as soon as possible! Skills: HTML, JavaScript, general Web design knowledge.

Careers in Web Design

While many Web designers are male, there are equal opportunities for women. A female Webmaster at Wal-Mart, the huge warehouse discount chain, says she is constantly looking for talented men and women "who can combine a lot of technical knowledge with the ability to cooperate with people who don't know a lot about technology."

Many companies first considered their Web site as a temporary experiment. Soon they learned the value of their Web site as a business and marketing essential. As more companies realize the benefits of having a Web site to promote their products and services, more people will be hired to create these sites.

The trend is also geared toward teams of skilled people to create Web sites. As technology becomes more sophisticated, with the addition of sound and movies to Web sites, those with more specialized skills are needed to create those sites. This same advanced technology is creating computer software to make it easier to create less sophisticated Web pages.

Some worry that because of easy-to-use Web design software, the job of a professional designer may no longer be in demand. Industry spokespeople suggest that this will not be the case because of the growing need for more sophisticated Web sites that are beyond the scope of do-it-yourself design. They also encourage Web designers to keep learning and using the latest technology in design and maintenance, and to be prepared for what is yet to come in the fast and ever changing world of the Internet.

Preparing for Your Web Career

A college education is not always necessary for a career as a Web designer. Instead, you can get a degree in computer science, which would include Web page design. Or you could study Web design at a college specializing in computer education. High school students can learn Web design if they do not plan to go to college. According to a *Web Week* magazine survey, most Web page designers and even Webmasters do not have formal, specific training in how to design Web sites. Some have bachelor's degrees, or two-year Web design certification degrees from technical schools, or just a high school diploma. The majority taught themselves the basic skills of designing Internet sites.

Education and Training

If You Plan to Go to College

You may not need a college degree to work as a Web designer, since many employers are more concerned that

Careers in Web Design

you know how to design a successful Web site. However, you could be a step ahead of the competition if you do get a college degree. It could be in computer science, a major in which students learn Web design and programming languages. Your degree could be in a subject related to computer technology or in a field related to Web design such as journalism, advertising, or graphic design. Those—plus technical knowledge of Web design—are the basic skills needed in creating a Web page. However, other Web designers may have education or training in mathematics, art, marketing, or engineering. Web design is a good career for those with a liberal arts degree and basic computer knowledge. You can learn computer technology, including Web design, and get a degree in computer science from many colleges and universities.

Typical of universities offering courses and degrees in Web design is the School of Computer Science, Telecommunications, and Information Systems at DePaul University in Chicago. Ten-week courses are offered each quarter in various branches of computer science, including Web design.

If you do not attend a traditional college or university, you could learn Web design at one of the many specialized computer schools located in most major cities. One example is Clark University's Computer Career Institute in Framingham, Massachusetts, which offers a certificate program in Web design and development.

At specialized computer schools such as Clark's, you learn to use the major tools for Web design, such as HTML, Dynamic HTML, and FrontPage. You also learn two major languages to develop rapid interactive applications for the Web—Java and Cold Fusion. Many young people who aspire to careers in Web design get a regular college education, then supplement it with a certificate in Web design from a computer school. Study may require either six weeks in the school's day program or about twenty weeks of part-time study evenings and Saturdays.

If You Are Not Going to College

After high school graduation, if you don't plan to go to college full-time, you can learn computer and Web design skills by taking part-time courses at community colleges or specialized computer technology schools. While it is not essential for Web designers to have a college degree, some employers prefer prospective employees to have a Webmaster certificate. Many computer or technical colleges offer certificates that show students have successfully completed training in Web design.

Develop Design Skills

Whether you get advanced schooling and training in Web design, one thing is certain: The more experience you have in design, the better.

What may impress a prospective employer more than a college degree is a sample of your ability to design a Web page. Begin early, while you are in high school, to create Web pages of various kinds and dealing with a variety of subjects. Learn to write well so you can create effective content. Effectively conveying information is one of the essentials of a successful Web site. The better writer you are, the better your content will read.

Add graphics to your Web pages by creating them yourself with artwork or photography, or find them from

THE ROSEN PUBLISHING GROUP

BOOKWORKS
1 2 3 4 5 6
YOUNG ADULT

POWER KIDS

REFERENCE

ROSEN BOOKWORKS
Publishers of reading material from beginning readers to young adult.

The art of composition makes a Web page attractive, dynamic, and easy to navigate.

the tens of thousands available in graphics software. Learn to resize pictures and alter their color or contrast. This is done using software such as Adobe PhotoShop.

"If your graphics look poor, your site will be unappealing," says Jean Kaiser, Web design authority for the free computer information site, About.com. "If your graphics are too large, your page's download time will suffer from being too long. Impatient viewers will just leave it."

Learn how to add links to a Web page. They should allow the viewer to find related material quickly, easily, and logically. The design "interface" allows users to navigate the Web page to find the specific information they want without wading through pages of lesser concern to them.

Learn the art of composition, which makes a Web page attractive, exciting, and easy to navigate. This involves skills in placing the various elements of the Web page, such as the content, graphics, and headings, in ways that make an attractive and logical composite.

Preparing for Your Web Career

Keep up with new technologies that add audio and visual effects as well as interactive features that enable users to communicate over the Internet. Besides technical skills, a Web designer needs both creativity and imagination to put together a successful page. Designers also need to develop the specialized skill of understanding what information and approach their employer wants on the Web site and what the people viewing it want to find on it.

Getting Started

You can practice learning skills in Web design while you are in high school. If you have access to a computer at home or school, practice Web design by using one of the sample Web pages and templates (patterns or guides) that are preinstalled in most word-processing software, such as Microsoft Word or Appleworks. Also, a simple search will lead you to sites that offer free Web design advice.

Web design software is also available for those who want to learn the basics, then add their own touches. One such program is Web Easy, a comprehensive Web page creation tool. You click on a background template, type the text you want to appear on your page, then use your mouse to drag and drop images from any source onto your page. You can select from scanned images, digital photos, or from a library of over fifty thousand templates, images, and clip art.

Practice designing Web pages by being creative with the samples and templates. Alter the basic page to add your own personal touches, which can make the text and graphics more appealing. Study a variety of Web sites on the Internet and see if the pages and links are easy and logical to navigate. While navigating the page, determine if it does what it is intended to do. Does it give the user the information that he or she went to the page hoping to find? Does the page convey the messages that the company or institution that had it created wants to communicate?

Maybe your school will let you help create pages for its Web site. Also, to gain experience, offer your Web design services free or for a modest fee to local organizations or small businesses. Experience is the key word in developing skills in Web design. As you gain more experience creating Web pages, be sure to store them on a disk. Also, print the Web pages and keep them in a file. Later, you can create a portfolio of your work to show to prospective employers as proof of your Web design skills.

Internships

One way to break into the Web design field is to get an internship. Some companies invite high school students or graduates to work from one to three months as part of a Webmaster team. In such an internship, you are given an opportunity to learn how to build a Web page on the job. The pay is usually low—and many internships are unpaid—but the experience you gain can be worth a lot.

Interns can store their Web work on-line and on disks to show prospective employers. They also may make connections with someone who will offer them a job, which is called networking. Many internships lead to full-time work with the same company.

Dan Trimble, cofounder and chief executive officer of an on-line computer information company called

Preparing for Your Web Career

Dantrimble.com, says, "Young people should get involved through internship programs. I can think of numerous students I've met and mentored who have gone through internship programs and have had life-changing experiences."

Trimble began his computer career at fourteen while a freshman at Terra Linda High School in San Rafael, California. "I entered a school-to-work program, working part-time for the Autodesk Foundation," says Trimble. "It's the nonprofit division of the PC software company Autodesk, Inc. I earned school credit as well as a salary."

After graduating from high school, Trimble became a full-time Autodesk employee, managing the company's Web programs and e-business operations. After three years, he started his own Web business. He was twenty-one years old. "I definitely suggest joining any company's information technology internship program," says Trimble. "Even while you're still in high school, you can get valuable experience and may even wind up working full-time for the company."

Researchers at Michigan State University's Career Services Placement department reported that employers place a high value on the work-related experience of recent college graduates. According to the department's study, 61 percent of employers rated credit-bearing internships as extremely important.

"We get hundreds of résumés," says Keith Kreiter, president of Edge Sports International, a Skokie, Illinois, firm that uses the Internet to help professional athletes decide which products—such as Coca-Cola or Nike—to endorse. "Unless you bring something extra to the table, you're not very attractive. It doesn't matter what college you went to or how many degrees you have. You need practical experience."

Kreiter helps young people get experience by hiring them in a semester-long internship program. One of his recent interns was Jack Harnedy, a senior in marketing at Northwestern University. "This has been an incredible experience for me," says Harnedy about the internship program. "In school, I learn a lot of theory. That's important. But this is definitely a real-world situation. It's nonstop here, every day."

Kathy Kessenich, manager of the internship programs and public information division of Rotary International, says, "Working before you get out of school, you're much more prepared for the demands of a profession. Once you've entered the work world and are trying to get a real job, an internship experience will be a great benefit."

To learn about the possibilities of Web-related internships in your area, ask your school counselor or job placement officer. Or write to a company you may be interested in working for, and ask if it has an internship program you might apply for.

How Internships Work

By taking part in an internship program, you not only gain professional skills, such as Web design, you also get insight into a particular industry and establish connections that might lead to a job. Human resources directors at companies hiring Web designers see internships as a training and testing ground for potential new employees. Says one human resources director, "Firms are spending more time and resources to develop internship programs because it provides them with an efficient way to cultivate future employees and weed out the less qualified."

Internships vary widely in the amount of pay or school credit offered, the type of supervision you receive, length of time you are expected to work, and the amount of learning you will be able to soak up. *InternshipPrograms.com*, a free on-line internship information service, says there are eight criteria you can use to understand and evaluate an internship you might be interested in.

1. Paid Versus Unpaid. Most paid internships are offered by major, well-financed corporations. Categories of businesses that offer the best salaries for interns are information technology, commercial banking, investment banking, consulting, accounting, venture capital, and marketing. Glamour industries such as entertainment and book publishing tend not to pay interns well or at all because so many young people clamor to get in their door. Still, almost all industries offer some paid internships to attract talented students at an early stage in their education. Some companies that do not pay interns may, however, give one-time stipends of $2,500 or more to help defray students' costs of living.

2. Credit Versus Not-for-Credit. Some colleges, hoping to steer students toward the real-world experience an internship provides, grant college credit for approved internships. Other cooperative education colleges and universities require students to do internships as part of their curriculum. Unfortunately, the majority of colleges do not award credit for internships.

3. **Mentor-Led Versus Self-Directed.** If you work best when you are on your own, an internship without a mentor (a counselor or experienced guide) can be a good thing. However, if you know you want to learn a certain job, such as Web design, but don't have the foggiest idea of how to go about doing it, then seek guidance from a mentor. Be sure your mentor has a clear understanding of what you would like to achieve and what your time frame for that is. Your mentor also should know how to structure your internship and track your progress throughout the project.

4. **Term-Time Versus Summertime.** Many internships are available to students only during their summer vacations. Companies and organizations want to ensure that they have enough work to keep you busy and don't want you to take valuable time away from your studies while interning. However, if you're interested in learning outside the classroom during the school year, and are confident your schoolwork won't suffer, then look for employers who hire interns all year around.

5. **Part-Time Versus Full-Time.** Two options exist for college students if they want long-term exposure to a particular company. The first option is to take a year or a semester off from college to take part in an internship program. The experience can be immensely rewarding for students; it also can provide a much needed break from

studies. Internships provide a chance for students to reexamine their career goals and focus the rest of their education. The second option is a part-time internship. This may not provide as clear a picture of what the daily demands are, but chances are you'll learn enough to decide whether or not you enjoy the work. Best of all, part-time internships don't require college students to take a year off, so you can still graduate with your classmates.

6. Cooperative Education. Another form of internship is a cooperative education program—a three-way partnership between a student, an employer, and a college or university. It allows students to integrate work experience into their academic studies for credit. Many colleges endorse "co-op education" by partnering with a variety of employers to provide career-related opportunities. Students in co-op education programs work in jobs that relate to their majors.

7. Externships. In externships, a high school or college graduate spends a short period of time, usually one to three weeks, observing and often working with professionals in his or her career field of interest. Young people experience a typical day on the job and observe the work environment and demands of the career. An externship is a good way to investigate a career field without making a commitment. However, externships are usually unpaid and are mainly in the medical and legal fields.

8. Apprenticeships. If you want to learn a highly skilled trade and earn money doing it, apprenticeships offer both practical experience and instruction. Apprenticeships are paid, and wages increase as the apprentice gains experience.

Apprenticeships used to last seven years. Today, apprenticeships vary in length from one to five years. Trades offering apprenticeships include electronics technology and the careers of Webmastering and graphic art. An example of a Web page design apprenticeship was the following, offered on-line by Hewlett-Packard, the computer equipment company.

Apprenticeship with Hewlett-Packard in Boise, Idaho. Become a member of a team working to improve the usability of a support Web site for worldwide users. Assist with usability studies and evaluations that provide consistent measures and suggest solutions to Web designers. Help in setting up usability lab to test effectiveness of Web sites.

To learn more about the wide range of internships, go on-line to *www.InternshipPrograms.com*. You can learn about possible internship or apprenticeship opportunities in Web design in your town or city by contacting local Web design firms. You can also find them listed in the yellow pages under Internet Services—Web Site Design and Developers. Contact companies or organizations in your area and ask about opportunities in their Web design department.

Technical Teens Internships

A highly regarded program offering information technology training to teenagers is the Technical Teens internship program. The intense three-year program, which offers hands-on training, including Web design, is a community effort of the Technology Access Foundation, a nonprofit organization in Seattle, Washington. "The program is geared toward high school students ages thirteen to eighteen who are interested in the field of information technology," says executive director Trish Millines. "Students can be in the program until they graduate from high school."

For eight months each year, students take information technology courses twice a week, three hours each session. Some sixty-eight students are currently in the internship program, working in a new work-study area they helped build. This consists of four PC labs; a Macintosh computer lab; a network lab with printers, scanners, and liquid crystal projectors; a resource room and library; a kitchen; and a break room. Classes run from October to May. June is reserved for interviewing for paid summer internships. At the end of each successful internship, each student gets a $1,000 scholarship toward college tuition.

Besides developing Web sites, "techteens" learn how to rebuild a computer, use operating systems and networks, use desktop software, and do schoolwork research on the Internet. Twice during the year, they work for an entire month developing Web sites and learn what it means to work on team projects.

In the first year of Technical Teens internships, students take twelve hours of instruction in computer hardware, twelve hours of Windows and networking, six hours of keyboarding, twelve hours of Word/Encarta, six hours of Internet basics and surfing the Web, thirty-six hours of HTML, twelve hours of JavaScript, twelve hours of job readiness and career development, and two month-long Web projects.

In the second year of the internship, students take thirty-two hours of networking, a month-long project installing a network, eighteen hours of media production, forty-two hours of server-side VBScript, a month-long Web project, and get a job readiness review. In the third year, students choose a track, or special field, of information technology they are interested in, such as Web development or network engineering. Plans are now underway for more choices, including media production and computer programming.

"There is a lot of interaction between techteens and professionals," says Sherry Williams, the program's coordinator. "They get to listen to corporate information technology specialists explain and teach what it really takes to work in a corporate environment and be a productive employee. They go on field trips to see first-hand what goes on in a high-tech company. On Parents' Night the teens get to show off their Web pages for family and friends. Their work is also put on the Internet so anyone anywhere in the world can see their Web page each year."

In order to be eligible for the internship program, students must have a grade point average of at least 2.5 and a working knowledge of English. The internships are open only to high school students living in or near Seattle, Washington. Learn more about Technical Teens by visiting their Web site at *www.techaccess.org*. If you

Internships generally involve many hours of computer instruction.

want to learn about possible internship programs in your area, ask your school's career guidance counselor or your local chamber of commerce.

International Telementor Center

One of the most extensive information technology mentoring programs for high school students is the International Telementor Center (ITC) program at the Center for Science, Mathematics and Technology Education (CSMATE) at Colorado State University in Fort Collins, Colorado. The program provides electronic mentoring relationships between students and adult professionals worldwide.

Traditional mentoring involves a one-on-one relationship in which an experienced person offers instruction to someone who wants to learn a certain skill. However, many talented and committed professionals such as those in information technology, including Web design, just don't have the time to spend with a student in a face-to-face mentoring program.

Many in the mentoring community have found the answer to be in "telementoring." By spending about thirty to forty-five minutes a week communicating with young people by e-mail, adult mentors can share their experience and expertise, helping students get higher grades and learn skills such as Web design. CSMATE has become the nonprofit home for the ITC, enabling busy professionals to make significant contributions to share their knowledge with teenagers utilizing computer and Internet technology.

The ITC was begun in 1995 by the Hewlett-Packard telementor program. Since then, it has served over 5,000 students in grades 5 through 12 and earned numerous awards. It is expected to serve at least 10,000 students worldwide each year by the year 2003.

Telementoring's special benefits are that it matches students with appropriate mentors without geographic limitation. Also, e-mail communication provides a means of connecting thousands of professionals with students on a scale that is impractical with traditional face-to-face mentoring. Students report that the telementoring experience is very worthwhile to them. They learn or improve their skills using computers, the Internet, and e-mail. Those receiving telementoring in Web design learn on-line what they may not have been able to from an in-person mentor.

Some of the information technology mentors in the ITC program are assisting high school students in the WebMaster School, a Web design lab school at Rochester Adams High School in Rochester Hills, Michigan.

"Students in our Web design program are now learning additional skills and problem solving by their e-mail relationships with professional Webmasters in other parts of the country," says Ceil Jensen, founder and director of the WebMaster School. "Essentially, a student defines a project by e-mail and ITC matches up a Webmaster who communicates via e-mail to walk the student through to accomplish the project or learn a solution to a problem. It would be impossible for them to get this mentoring help except from the telementoring program at ITC."

Computer Industry Internships

Many companies involved in the information technology industry offer internships to high school and college students. Young people learn computer skills at the companies, including Web page design, and the industry helps provide much-needed, experienced people for the present and future workforce.

Hewlett-Packard, one of the major manufacturers of computer equipment, is a leader in providing internships through which young people learn about Web design and other information technology. In 1997, Hewlett-Packard and the Hewlett-Packard Company Foundation committed $5 million over five years to a new Diversity in Education Initiative (DEI).

The program supports four university and K-12 school partnerships that initiate or expand effective programs serving African American, Native American, and Latino students. Partnerships in Boston, El Paso, Los Angeles, and San Jose were awarded DEI grants to support partnership work from 1997 through 2002.

Sixty college freshmen and sophomore engineering or computer science students from Hewlett-Packard's three DEI partnerships are awarded a scholarship of $3,000 per year for four years of college. They are also offered paid summer internships at Hewlett-Packard during each of the three summers between their years of engineering studies. Each Hewlett-Packard scholar is matched with a Hewlett-Packard e-mail mentor who helps him or her prepare a résumé, get ready for interviews, and prepare for his or her summer internship experience.

One of the Hewlett-Packard scholars, Dare Oyedele, was born in Nigeria. He came to the United States with his parents after they relocated in Boston when he was five years old. He was in a Hewlett-Packard internship program in Palo Alto, California. An enthusiastic young man, he e-mailed an assessment of his internship learning about Web design.

Preparing for Your Web Career

"I'm currently a sophomore majoring in computer science at Northeastern University in Boston. I just turned twenty years old. While in high school at Boston Latin School, my work with Web design consisted only of developing a few static pages in my systems applications class using DreamWeaver, which introduced me to basic HTML.

The summer of my senior year, I learned more about HTML for a project to develop a Web site for Boston Renaissance Charter School. It wasn't until my current Hewlett-Packard internship that I produced Web work seen by others. The Web site was a modified copy of an existing Web site to fit the needs of an upcoming job fair.

The Web site was to implement a part of Hewlett-Packard's telementoring program. It was interactive, combining JavaScript and VBScript. Its interactivity allowed company managers to sign up for telementoring interview times with students.

Although I possessed neither the knowledge nor the understanding of the technology prior to the internship, I was able to learn it immediately. The majority of my internship is focused on developing and maintaining databases. Setting up the job fair Web site introduced me to a new and growing side of HTML. Working with Hewlett-Packard is an extremely good opportunity, since it gives you the exposure and chance to work in the technology field at a young age. An internship experience helps you decide whether a career is right for you. You also learn the skills needed to be successful, skills that may not be taught in the classroom.

I got the internship because I'm a Hewlett-Packard Diversity in Education Initiative (DEI) scholar. The high school I attended is one of the schools where Hewlett-Packard targets minority and female students who plan on majoring in a technical field—such as engineering or computer science. If accepted, the students are given a four-year scholarship. Part of the criteria is serving three summer internships with Hewlett-Packard, and they help us locate available positions for the summer.

For those who plan on a career in Web design, it is no longer enough to know HTML. More and more Web sites require moderate programming skills. These add such elements as Java and VBScript to produce dynamic and interactive Web pages. Web technology is still growing, so it's necessary to learn new skills and advanced technology in Web design.

I'm uncertain at present as to what my future career will be, although I believe it will be in some aspect of information technology. My current interest is to explore the networking field. Besides a strong career interest in networking, which involves Web design and computer programming, I would also like to improve the overall reading skills among deaf youth, because their average *reading level is extremely low. The reason I'm focusing specifically on deaf youth is because I am deaf.*

Dare Oyedele's internship in Web design may lead him to a career that combines his interest in information technology with networking to find ways to improve the reading skills of the hearing impaired. His goal is just one of seemingly endless examples of how information technology, including the Internet, is changing the work and personal lives of millions. For more information on Hewlett-Packard's internship program, go on-line to the Hewlett-Packard K-12 Web site, *www.hp.com/go/k12*, and the Hewlett-Packard Scholars Web site, *www.hp.com/go/hpscholars*.

Most information technology companies offer internship programs to high school and college students, and many of them teach Web design and development skills. To learn more about internship opportunities in information technology, go to *www.acm.org/student/internships.html*. There you will find listings and links to over a dozen companies with internship opportunities in computer technology that may include Web design. Companies include Apple Computer Corporation, AT&T, Compaq Computers, Dell Computers, Electronic Data Corporation, Gateway Computers, GTE Laboratories, IBM, Intel, Microsoft, Sun Microsystems, and Texas Instruments.

Learn Web Design in High School

Maybe your high school is one of the many that has a computer lab where you can learn computer skills such as using the Internet and e-mail to do course research. Some schools have special Web design programs teaching HTML, JavaScript, graphics and multimedia features. Also, some high school computer learning programs are affiliated with local or national companies that offer internships.

The WebMaster School

One of the most advanced high school computer education programs is the WebMaster School at Adams High School in Rochester Hills, Michigan. The program offers Web page design for selected local and national businesses as well as instruction in basic Internet use. Besides learning basic computer skills, students enrolled in the WebMaster School get hands-on training in all phases of designing Web pages. Room 200 at Adams High is equipped with Internet-connected computers, scanning equipment, digital cameras, and the latest editions of Web design software such as Microsoft FrontPage and graphics software such as Adobe PhotoShop.

Ceil Jensen, a social studies teacher at Adams High, started the WebMaster School in 1996 by writing the curriculum for the class, then applying for donations and grants to launch it. The appeal brought in $89,000. The largest contribution was $50,000 from California's school-to-work program, which supports projects that showcase how schools can collaborate with businesses to prepare students for the workplace.

Jensen used the grant money to buy software and add a dozen multimedia computers to the computer lab. The classroom mimics a business setting, with a conference table for client meetings separated from the main classroom area by a low wall. Students wear ties or dresses when clients come calling and hand out business cards they make with a laser printer.

"Webmastering is the only career that requires all the characteristics a creative student possesses and merges them with an intense marketplace need," says Jensen. "The Webmaster curriculum is designed so that visual art students, creative writers, techies, and budding entrepreneurs can work together as a team to create Web sites for real clients. They are using the tools of the twenty-first century to gain experience for jobs in one of the fastest growing careers in information technology."

The WebMaster School's first clients were twelve local companies that were recruited with the aid of the Greater Rochester Chamber of Commerce. Those agreeing to hire students to create Web sites for their business included a building contractor, a community group that wanted a Web site for its newsletter, a bike shop, and a nonprofit youth service agency. After the Web sites were created, they appeared free on an Internet server, courtesy of other backers, the local *Observer* and *Eccentric* newspapers.

In return for its Web site, each company donated $500 to the class and gave students some expertise by mentoring them in their particular area of work. Hiring professional Web designers would have cost each company thousands of dollars.

Starting fall semester 1996, students organized into six teams, each serving two clients. They spent the first two months in the program learning Web design software graphics and the tools to automate programming in HTML. They then met with their clients, studied their businesses and needs, and roughed out plans for the Web sites.

By December, the teams were rushing to complete Web designs, scan photographs, assemble the text, and get clients' approval of their work. "We had actual people counting on us," says Lael Ohdner, who was then part of the program. "Sometimes you had a week where the client was coming next Monday, and you had to finish working on the Web site."

By the end of the semester, all twelve Web sites were up and running, although still under construction. Depending on the skills of the team, some sites were basic one-page calling cards, while others were more complex and had links to various parts of a company's business. "The luckiest client was Wahu! bicycle company," says Jensen. "The top Web designer in the class, David Moffitt, scanned the bicycle manufacturer's catalog and added it to the Web site, using his home computer."

The WebMaster School, unlike traditional school-based enterprises, did not grow out of a vocational program. It is an art elective class officially called Visual Communication. A course in art fundamentals is a prerequisite. Marcia Gibbens, director of curriculum for the Rochester school district, enthusiastically supports the WebMaster School project. Says Gibbens, "The course exemplifies what the whole school-to-work movement is, by getting business people into the classroom and students into workplaces."

The National Association of Webmasters also endorses the WebMaster School. "The course is consistent with our research as to the skills that employers are requesting of Web designers today," says the association's executive director, William Cullifer. "It helps students develop skills that are in demand through its focus on technical know-how, content management, and business management."

"The course offers students work-based learning opportunities," says Jensen. "Career development plans are presented by college representatives and information technology specialists. They describe college majors in Webmastering as well as related careers in visual communication and art direction. After WebMaster School, students learn the various skills involved in Web design. They create their own site to demonstrate their abilities. At the end of the twenty-week class they are assessed on their student portfolio, public exhibition of their Web site, and student and client critiques."

A strong supporter of the WebMaster School is David S. Stern, professor of education at the University of California, Berkeley. "Offering Web-related study programs is a new wrinkle in the well-established idea of school-based enterprises," says Stern.

WebMaster School students also like the course. Kendra Waldrep, seventeen, says the WebMaster course pushed her in the right direction. "For a long time, I had wanted to be a teacher," says Waldrep. "But when I took the WebMaster course, the whole computer world opened up for me." She designed a Web site for Sanctuary, a local shelter for runaway teens.

Michael Coury, sixteen, says he has signed up to take the next WebMaster course because it offers a place to learn the technical aspects of Web design as well as gain business experience. "Fortunately, the companies that hire us are willing to give us a chance, put up with our mistakes, and let us wet our feet in the real world."

Jonathan Green, sixteen, gained knowledge and experience by just hanging around the WebMaster classroom. "I knew I loved computers but never really thought I could make a living at it." After learning the basics of Web design, he began doing freelance Web site development and working as an intern at a local high-tech company.

After four years, there are now one hundred alumni of the WebMaster School. A growing number of these are now experienced Web designers, who either gained expertise while still in school or in full-time jobs after graduation. "There's nothing wrong with working at McDonald's," says one WebMaster student. "But you can get paid a lot more for building a Web site!"

Besides creating Web sites for clients, WebMaster students are running digital workshops for local groups whose members want family Web pages. The students show adults how to scan, enlarge, and enhance old family photos and create multimedia files for their Web sites. Another new project is setting up a site for Adams High class reunions. The plan is to get local businesses to advertise on the reunion home page to welcome alumni back to town. Early in 2000, Jensen began plans to launch the WebMaster School into a project to create a Web site with a databank that will help a national organization in its efforts to feed the hungry. The students will work with ResourceLink on the databank, which will allow foodbanks to request perishables in a matter of minutes.

"WebMaster School has outgrown its initial role as a local school-to-work program," says Jensen. "A new frontier is needed for these creative, motivated, and impressionable high school students. What a match in the food-for-the-hungry program!

"Techno-savvy teens are mentoring civic-minded adults on how to navigate the Internet to bring resources where they're needed. It will align with national standards for high school technology, school-to-work, and community service. More important, in an era when hacking and pirating are attractive on-line sports, these teens will be part of a technology delivery system that demonstrates corporate giving," says Jensen.

For more information about the WebMaster School, visit *www.rochester-hills.com*. (The Web design students created the school's Internet page.) Your local high school may have a similar program in learning how to design a Web page. If it doesn't, ask the director of your school's computer lab if one can be started.

Plugged-In Enterprises

Another program that gives teenagers valuable experience in Web design is Plugged-In Enterprises. Established in 1992, it is a nationally recognized community computer center in California. Plugged-In operates three programs: the Technology Access Center, the Plugged-In Greenhouse, and Plugged-In Enterprises.

The Technology Access Center is a cross between a library, a self-paced computer skills learning studio, and a copy center. It is open to members of the community seventy hours a week. Plugged-In Greenhouse is a technology-based afterschool program for children to learn computer skills. Plugged-In Enterprises (PIE) is a Web design business run by teenagers living in East Palo Alto, California. High school students spend from ten to fourteen hours a week after school learning Web design skills. They learn design and technology, then practice these skills in developing Web sites for local and national companies and organizations. Clients include Hewlett-Packard, Pacific Bell, and Sun Microsystems.

Technical training at Plugged-In Enterprises focuses on computer basics, introduction to graphic design using Adobe PhotoShop, and HTML coding. In the training, students benefit from the expertise and experience of a wide range of professionals working at Silicon Valley computer companies. Volunteers from *Wired* magazine, Intel Corporation, Crystal Dynamics, Stanford University School of Education, Cisco Systems, Macromedia, and Sun Microsystems share their talents with the East Palo Alto teens.

"Thirty-six teenagers participate in the Web design program each year," says Magda Escobar, executive director of Plugged-In Enterprises. "They operate a Web production business and develop Web sites for paying clients, earning money for their work. Their work is evaluated by their supervisors and critiqued by their clients, and they are encouraged to keep abreast of new developments in Web design."

The teens' hourly pay is dependent on their skill level and their ability to transfer skills to peers on the production team as well as to other teens in the community. Several of the teens tell why they signed on to the Plugged-In Enterprises program and what it is doing or has done for them.

"I started at Plugged-In Enterprises when I was a freshman and have been in the program almost four years," says Dominic Bannister Jr., who lives in East Palo Alto. "I started coming to Plugged-In when I attended a class called StreetNet. Then I applied for a summer job at Plugged-In Enterprises. I learned how to answer telephones and do technical work. After the summer ended, I was asked to join Plugged-In Enterprises. I learned how to design a Web page and worked with applications like Adobe PhotoShop, Adobe PageMill, Infini-D, Gif Builder, and Fetch. I want to become a computer programmer. Working for Plugged-In Enterprises is a step toward my future goal. What keeps me in the program is the attention I get when I do something excellent."

Bannister says he was open to the opportunity of learning Web design, but not everyone else is. "I think Plugged-In has opened up opportunities for many teens, but they are not taking advantage of it. This reminds me of a quote:'You can't wait for your future to come to you, you have to plan for the future.'"

Bannister recently graduated from high school and began working full-time as a lead Web designer at Plugged-In Enterprises. "I want to own my own company someday," says Bannister. "In pursuit of my dreams, I will be attending San Francisco State University in the fall. I am very excited."

A fellow Plugged-In Enterprises student, Weslina Fort, also from East Palo Alto, says she first became interested in the program by going to the Technology Access Center to learn about computers. "It was a place that I liked to spend some of my free time," says Fort.

After several years of working at Plugged-In Enterprises while in high school, she graduated and is attending a local college majoring in computer science. "Working for Plugged-In Enterprises has been beneficial to me because I have learned Web design programs such as HTML, DreamWeaver, and Adobe PhotoShop, and I am currently learning Macromedia Flash. Being at Plugged-In Enterprises has helped me achieve personal goals. After college, I plan to open my own business dealing with computers."

Another teen working and learning at Plugged-In Enterprises, John Mireles, has a strong interest in art and design. "I am on a graphic design team at Plugged-In Enterprises," says Mireles. "I've always had an interest in the arts. I paint, sculpt, and sketch." Through his work at Plugged-In Enterprises, Mireles got a summer internship with a local design firm. "I feel the program not only is giving me a more promising future, but a better present. It is also a place for me to feel creative and express myself."

To learn more about Plugged-In Enterprises, go to *www.pluggedin.org*. To review a portfolio of the work the teens have accomplished at Plugged-In Enterprises, go to *www.pluggedin.org/pie* and click the "Portfolio" link.

Explore the Web

One of the best ways to learn about Web sites, and how they are designed to do various things, is to go on-line and study them. "Look at the source codes of pages that you like," suggests Jean Kaiser, who hosts a design Web site for *About.com*. "Check the top of the source code to be sure the pages were not set using a cheap ready-made type of editor. Then save the pages onto your hard drive and open them in Notepad.

"Take the pages apart and see how they work. Make changes and see what happens. You can make changes and view the pages on your hard drive through your browser by going to the file menu and clicking on 'Open Page.' This is a good hands-on way to get a feel for what HTML does." Kaiser also suggests studying the design and navigation of Web sites you like. "Look for sites that are easy to navigate as well as pleasing in design. Figure out what makes these sites work. This will help you decide on a layout for your own site. Determine where your graphics and text will go. Consider where users will want to go in your site and how they can get there."

The following is a sampling of various types of Web sites, from the moderately simple to more complex, interactive sites.

A Small Business Web Site

Bernard Schmidt, who builds homes in the suburbs north of Chicago, tells why he had a Web site designed for his business. "I advertise in local newspapers but wanted to reach prospective home buyers throughout Illinois and across the nation. I hired a freelance Web site designer who put Schmidt and Associates on-line and immediately began attracting customers."

Schmidt's Web site has links that let home buyers learn about his construction company, see his photo, and read a welcome message by him. They then can link to options such as viewing a gallery of his already-built homes, which include single-family and town homes. Another link leads to vacation homes the company builds in Galena, a resort community several hundred miles west of Chicago. The site also includes addresses of vacant lots the company can build new homes on, design features, contact information, and other links.

"We know the trend in advertising and marketing just about everything is toward having a presence on the Internet," says Schmidt. "It is becoming commonplace for people to search the Web to look for realtors and construction companies in the area where they want their new home built. Our site lets prospective home buyers all over the country check us out from the comfort and convenience of their home."

To see how Schmidt and Associates' Web site looks, go to *www.schmidtassoc.com*. Study what's there, how the text and photos were placed, and how the links lead to a logical, complete, on-line tour of a residential construction business.

A Corporate Web Site

Ford Motor Company, one of the giants in the automotive industry, has a more complex Web site offering links to various interests of auto and truck buyers. An "Our Products" link takes viewers to parts of the site that let them browse, build, or buy new and pre-owned vehicles, merchandise, and accessories. Options invite viewers to select a brand and model to see photos and read about Ford, General Motors, and Daimler-Chrysler vehicles. Links lead car buyers to select types of vehicles such as small passenger cars, midsize cars, sports cars, and luxury cars.

Links also take viewers to information on owner benefits, auto service, financing, and career opportunities at the auto manufacturers. Company news regarding new lines of cars and trucks, and new developments in environment and safety features are also found on the site. Another link leads to sites about auto merchandise and accessories. The Ford Motor Company Web site is a good one to check out to see how its designers presented extensive information in a rather simple way. The address is *www.ford.com*.

A Museum Web Site

Some of the most interesting Web sites are those for museums. One of these is the Smithsonian Institution in Washington, DC. The Smithsonian's site invites on-line museum-goers to visit the Museum and Research Centers, Educational Outreach, Libraries and Archives, Events and Activities, and New Exhibitions. Links to the Institution's various museums include the main building, called the Castle; the Arts and Industries Building; the Center for African-American History and Culture; and the Smithsonian Center for Latino Initiatives.

One of the most popular areas on the Smithsonian site is the National Air and Space Museum. On-line visitors can visit the Apollo to the Moon exhibition to access exhibits on America's mission to the moon. Much can be learned about sophisticated design by visiting the Smithsonian on-line at *www.si.edu*.

A Government Web Site

The National Aeronautic and Space Agency (NASA) has a very popular Web site from which a great deal can be learned about design. "NASA is deeply committed to spreading the unique knowledge that flows from its aeronautics and space research departments," says NASA administrator Daniel G. Goldin in a welcome address at the Web site. Recent news of America's space program and a searchable archive of recent and past NASA activities are to be found in photos, text, and audio-video presentations.

In links regarding space travel, students who view the space agency's Web site learn about NASA rocket classroom activities. They include information on the history of rockets and rocket principles and how to make a rocket pinwheel and paper rocket.

Multimedia galleries include access to NASA photographs, a video gallery featuring digital video, and animation related to NASA and space exploration. An audio gallery allows access to NASA's radio broadcasts. NASA's Web site is located at *www.nasa.com*.

A Movie Review Web Site

Stylish graphics can often be found on on-line movie review Web sites, such as *Amazon.com*'s Internet Movie Database. Information on thousands of movies—new and old—are cross-referenced by title, players, director, and plot. Viewers also access links to reviews of the week's top five movies as well as other movies currently playing. A brief summary of each movie is given, as well as short reviews written by fans who play "movie critic."

The Web site also offers links to movie-related games, contests, and message boards in which viewers exchange comments on movies and stars. The site's fun features invite viewers to learn what famous people share their birthday and participate in on-line polls, and includes extensive star biographies and filmographies. Visit the Internet Movie Database at *www.imdb.com*.

A Multimedia Web Site

One of the most advanced multimedia Web sites is found at *Shockwave.com*, a showcase of both Macromedia Flash technology and the latest Web design trends. The site includes popular classic arcade video games such as Tetris and Centipede, classic card games, cartoon downloads (including *South Park*), and animated e-mail greeting cards. *Shockwave.com* can be studied for its use of state-of-the-art multimedia technology. You need to have the most current version of the Macromedia Flash plug-in installed on your computer to fully experience this site, but it is easy, fast, and free to download and install Macromedia Flash directly from the site.

An Interactive Web Site

A very popular interactive Web site specifically for teens is *About.com*'s Teen Advice Forum. At the Teen Advice Forum, teens can scroll to a subject of special interest such as career planning or dating advice. A click on the site's message board invites viewers to read and respond to current on-line discussions among teens. You can post your views on a subject or ask for guidance on questions that matter to you. Popular topics have included "How do I get my crush?" "What are some bad things happening at school?" and "Is it okay to cry?" Almost as soon as a question is posted on the bulletin board, replies come

Careers in Web Design

in that anyone can then reply right back to. It's like a telephone conversation with teens from all over the world—except that it's on-line.

There are also links to helpful information on topics of interest to teens such as "Dating Manual for Guys." There are also links to chat groups and finding pen pals to communicate with on-line. The Teen Advice Forum demonstrates how interesting interactive Web sites can be. The site is located at *www.delphi.com/ab-teenadvice/start*. These Internet sites are just a few examples of the most advanced Web design technology. They give a solid indication of what effective Web sites must contain.

Section II
Working as a Web Designer

Getting Your First Job

There are basically three types of workplaces for Web designers:

1. You can work as a Web designer as a full-time salaried staff member of a company that uses Web sites to promote their business.
2. You can work for a Web development company, creating Web sites for other companies.
3. You can be a self-employed, or freelance, Web designer, finding your own clients.

Essentially, the work is the same no matter if you work for someone or are a freelancer. Your job is to create a Web site for a client who most likely will have one or more products or services to market. In this chapter you will meet people who work as Web designers in each of the three job categories. While their work may be very similar, their working conditions, salaries, benefits, and other aspects of their work may differ.

Designing Web Sites

One person may design a Web site, or two or more people may work as a team. Large and complex sites often require the talents of a staff of writers, graphic designers, and programmers who work in a company's Web development department.

In large companies, the Web department may include one or more designers and developers, a Webmaster who acts as a supervising manager, a computer and Internet technology expert, a graphics designer, an information architect, and one or more content developers. In smaller companies or on smaller Web design jobs, one person may do the work of an entire Web department.

In a sense, every person who designs a Web site by themselves is also a Web developer and a Webmaster. The Webmaster's Guild (*www.webmaster.org*) says, "The goal of a Webmaster is to design, implement, and maintain an effective Web site. To achieve this, a Webmaster must possess knowledge of fields as diverse as network configuration, interface and graphic design, software development, business strategy, writing, marketing, and project management. Because the function of a Webmaster encompasses so many areas, the position is often held not by a single person but by a team of individuals."

Internet and Intranet Sites

Many larger companies have two types of Web sites: Internet sites and Intranet sites. An Internet site is one available to anyone anywhere in the world via the Web. They are the sites companies use to advertise and sell their products and services. An Intranet site is available only to employees of the company. It is an internal means by which employers communicate with their employees right at their office computer. Intranet Web sites contain corporate news and other information that otherwise would be given out by telephone or in memos. In each case, Web designers create and maintain Internet sites, but with either external or internal company focus.

In the following pages, the focus will be on the work of Web designers of Internet sites. Common responsibilities of Web designers/developers are to:

— Create a Web site that effectively conveys what a client wants to promote or sell. The site should load fast and be easy to navigate.
— Publish the Web site on the Internet so the maximum number of potential customers know about the site and can access it easily.
— Maintain the Web site and periodically add new content as required by the client.

Differences in Jobs

The main differences in who you work for as a Web designer involve hours, working conditions, salary, and benefits. If you work full-time for a company developing its site or for a Web development firm you are a salaried employee entitled to benefits such as health insurance and retirement guarantees. You also will be required to keep regular office hours which are usually 9 AM to 5 PM Monday through Friday. Depending on the employer, dress code may vary wildly from traditional to extremely casual. Web companies are leaders in the trend toward more flexible office hours and more casual dress codes.

If you work as a freelancer, you may still get paid well but will not receive health, retirement, or other benefits because you are not considered a full-time employee. Your number of working hours may still conform to those of your employer, but they may not be as long and inflexible as they would if you were a salaried employee. But you may find yourself working nights and weekends to make up for working fewer hours at the company. If you do your work at home, the dress code and hours are up to you.

Financial benefits of working at a home office can be tax deductions for the workroom portion of your apartment or home, which includes rent, mortgage, utilities, as well as deductible auto and travel expenses. A major benefit of being a self-employed Web designer is that although you will have to spend time learning what your client wants its site to contain and how it will look and navigate, you can do the actual work at home. Freelancers avoid the pressure of an employer closely watching them as they work. The end result, however, must be satisfactory—a Web site that does what the client pays you to create. And you may have to do more of the development tasks yourself, rather than work with others who may be specialists in one or more aspects of design. A benefit from working alone can be more personal control over the creation of the Web site.

What may help you decide between working for a company or freelancing is how independent you are and how disciplined you are. Working at home can be distracting and any number of things can take you away

Practice your interviewing skills with a friend to prepare yourself for the real thing.

from the task at hand, from walking the dog to repairing a leak in the roof. Most people work better and more efficiently in a controlled office environment without everyday living distractions.

Steps Toward Your First Job

While in high school or computer trade school attend any job or career fairs that are held, to learn of job openings after graduation or certification as a Web developer. Most schools have job counselors or placement officers to help students who are close to graduation in their job hunting. After graduation, there are six ways to search for your first job in Web design:

1. Write a résumé of your education and experience. A sample résumé will be found following this list, and books are available in libraries to help you write an effective résumé.

2. Test your skills at being interviewed by a prospective employer. Ask a parent or friend to pretend they are interviewing you for a job as a Web designer so you can practice convincing a future employer about your abilities. Books are also available to help you develop interviewing skills.

3. Network. Contact any people you know who might give you a recommendation for a job.

4. Study newspaper and on-line help wanted notices for entry-level design positions.

5. Practice writing a short cover letter to send to a prospective employer with your résumé. The cover letter should briefly summarize your education, experience or qualifications, and specify the work for which you are applying.

6. Submit your résumé to an on-line computer job search service such as *ComputerJobs.com* or *Monster.com*. These Web-based recruitment agencies maintain databases of résumés and jobs in different regions of the United States and the rest of the world, and they cover many different skill categories, including Web design.

Sample Résumé

A high school student's and a college student's résumé will differ mainly in education and experience. *Internship Programs.com* offers the following suggestions for a college student's scannable résumé and a sample résumé.

When you submit your résumé via fax, e-mail, or snail mail to most large companies, it is scanned into their résumé database. Department heads such as those in charge of the company's communications department periodically search the database for key words that describe concepts or characteristics within the résumés that match the job they want to fill. If your résumé includes the right keywords, then it is viewed by the person who is doing the hiring.

A scannable résumé should not include fancy text, bullets, underlines, or columns. If you already have them in your résumé, take them out. Your résumé can best help you land a job if it is written simply, in a plain text editor such as Notepad, WordPad, or a text document in Microsoft Word. Follow these steps:

1. Place your name and contact information at the top of the page.
2. Insert a paragraph of keywords that describe your abilities and characteristics.
3. Add experience, education, etc., using caps to label the sections.
4. Try to keep the résumé to just one page.

Most job placement agencies throughout the country can help you in your search for work as a Web designer. The more experience you can describe in your résumé, the better your chances of getting the job you want. Remember, however, that it is both unlawful and unethical to lie on your résumé.

Josephine Smith
1234 Main Street
Smalltown, IL 60654
(847) 555-5555
e-mail: jintern@hotline.com

EDUCATION
Graduating June 2001 with bachelor's degree in computer science from Northern Illinois University. GPA 3.2/4.0
Received special class award for excellence in Web design and maintenance.
Relevant courses: Computer science, Web design, accounting, marketing, micro- and macroeconomics, money and banking.

EXPERIENCE
Internship, Microsoft Corporation, Summer 2000.
Worked as part of a Web development team to establish new marketing channels for products.

Internship, Hewlett-Packard Corporation, Summer 1999.
Helped design and implement a new advertising campaign for a Web site promoting a new line of printers.

Part-time caddy, Municipal Golf Course, Summer 1998.
Starter and pro-shop attendant. Ran cash register and audited end-of-day receipts.

ACTIVITIES
Assistant editor of daily college newspaper.
Member of college computer club.
Member of varsity tennis and soccer teams.
Computer and filing work in school business office ten hours per week.

SPECIAL SKILLS
Computers, Internet, Netscape, Internet Explorer, e-mail, fax, HTML, JavaScript, PhotoShop, Web design, e-commerce, advertising, marketing.

Getting Your First Web Design Job

Randy Ksar, who designs and develops Web sites for Sony Electronics in California, offers advice on how to get a job creating Web sites:

> *The first step in getting a job designing Web sites is to learn what the work involves. Is it all site programming or does it require a little marketing knowledge? Actually, it involves both.*
>
> *To maximize your job performance, you need to have a good background in Web programming as well as marketing and business. Web designers don't spend all day at the computer screen hacking at code (creating pages in HTML or other design language). Their usual day is spent meeting with clients and figuring out a good strategy on implementing their advertising campaign on the Web.*
>
> *Designing a Web site is only part of your work. If a customer asks you to build a site, you should know who to contact in order to maximize the customer's presence on the Internet.*
>
> *Know who to contact if you don't know the answer to a question or how to solve a problem. Many Web design experts are on-line to help you. Never tell a client, 'I don't know.' Tell them, 'I'll get right back to you on that,' and then get help."*

Ksar says that to be a successful Web designer, keeping in touch with technology is a must. Reading up on the material through the Web or through magazines such as *Web Week* is very helpful. "Every weekend, read up-to-date computer-related periodicals and in a few months you can impress your boss and clients," says Ksar. "Read about the latest HTML features. It will definitely pay off. All you need is a little time and patience." It is not necessary to know the in-depth details of the technology, but at least to know the capabilities—what the technology can do to help you in developing Web sites.

Designing the Web site is just the first step. Maintaining the site can be an ongoing job requiring just as much or more skill and time. The most effective Web sites are those that change and are updated at least monthly and many require weekly or even daily additions or changes. Prices of selling products or services on-line may change rapidly, or new products are introduced while those from inventory that do not sell well are discontinued or relegated farther back on a Web site. New technologies may be introduced to make the Web site more exciting or just faster to navigate.

Because Web sites should not remain unchanged, more work is assured for developers and those who maintain the sites. In the following chapters you will meet those who are salaried Web designers and developers and those who are self-employed. Some work by themselves, some as part of teams. All share the common goal of designing Web pages that get more "hits" (visitors to the site) than the competition.

Meet Web Designers/Developers

You can work at a wide range of companies as a full-time salaried Web designer or as a self-employed freelance designer. The work is essentially the same whether salaried or freelance. You have to create a Web site that does what the client wants it to do.

Some of the sites you will develop will be to sell a company's product or service, while others may be for colleges and universities, public service organizations, or government agencies. Whatever your commercial or social service interests are, you can likely find work. The following are a few examples of people who find job satisfaction designing sites for a variety of employers or freelancing.

A Web Site Selling a Product

Cyrus Khoshnevisian designs the company site for Peter Granoff, who sells wine over the Internet through his firm, Wine.com (*www.wine.com*). Khoshnevisian says he and other Web designers are becoming increasingly aware of the need to make their sites faster to navigate.

Web design teams must be innovative and creative to keep up with their competitors.

Although selling products and services over the Internet is a relatively new marketing tool, competition has grown quickly. This means Web sites have to "tell and sell" faster. The wine industry is just one example of this.

"Web site speed is of paramount importance," says Granoff. "There's a natural tendency for Americans to get things done fast, and they're willing to embrace new technology that makes it possible."

Khoshnevisian agrees: "My Web design staff and I are constantly looking for ways in which we can leverage the technology. It's a never-ending process. Any e-commerce company worth its dot-com is engaged in a similar endeavor."

To help his Webmaster speed up *Wine.com*'s Internet presence, Granoff hired Keynote, the first of a growing number of Web performance measurement companies. Their mission is to help get Web sites up to speed. Keynote is now part of a new Internet industry to measure, assess, and suggest ways to improve ease of navigation and Web design. "Performance" has become almost synonymous with speed—the time it takes a customer to load the first page of a Web site, to link to another page, or to buy something such a case of wine.

Umang Gupta, the head of Keynote, based in San Mateo, California, knows the importance of speed in navigating a Web site. "If you go to *Amazon.com* or *Barnesandnoble.com*, there's not much difference in selection, or in the look and feel of their Web pages. The difference comes down to speed—the speed of downloading or the speed of delivery."

Zona Research, hired by Keynote to assess the importance of speed in navigating Web sites, reported: "On the Internet, the need for speed is a fact of life. In almost every way imaginable, speed rules."

The report cited the "eight-second rule," a widely held belief that customers will leave a Web site if the download time exceeds eight seconds. It estimated that Internet companies in the United States lose more than $4 billion each year from purchases that are not made because customers found certain Web sites too slow.

Service Metrics, another firm that tracks Web site speed, monitors the performance of specific sites within a particular industry during their most crucial selling periods. They found that among on-line tax consulting Web sites, Yahoo Tax Center was the fastest, averaging 1.65 seconds to download the first page. The slowest was *1040.com,* whose first on-line page took 13.97 seconds to download. Seconds count in on-line selling. For Mother's Day, Service Metrics determined that the download time for FTD Flowers' Web site was two-thirds of a second faster than 1-800-Flowers, its chief rival.

A Web Page Development Firm

Many companies, organizations, and institutions do not have staff people creating and maintaining their Web sites. Instead, they hire the services of a Web development firm. One such service firm is Voyager Information Networks, Inc. Kevin Johnson, the company's Web site administrator, talks about his duties.

"I'm responsible for our company's Web site layout and design, reporting to the creative services director. I work with the Web sales staff and meet with clients to discuss design and content. I also assist in preparing proposals for clients who want us to develop their Web sites. A very important part of my job is to keep informed of technology developments involving Web design and maintenance."

Johnson's work is part technical, part people-related. He keeps summaries of progress being made to satisfy the agreements in client contracts regarding development of their Web sites. He maintains a log of work done for each task in that development. Salaries for the employees of Web development firms range from $30,000 to $50,000.

A Company's Intranet Web Site

Keeping in communication with employees within a large corporation used to be done by printing newsletters, sending memos, or holding meetings. Today it's faster and more efficient for companies to communicate with employees within and between departments by means of an internal Web site, called the Intranet.

After earning a certificate in computer programming from a two-year business college, Nancy Cooper worked for a Web development firm for five years. She then became a Web developer for the internal communications of a national multiservice insurance company. "Our company's Intranet went live in January 2000," says Cooper. "Everyone's roles are continually evolving, but a general structure has been established."

The company has five divisions and each has a Webmaster who is responsible for developing and maintaining that division's Web site. Since each division has a different function, what each Webmaster is responsible for changes frequently. However, the division Webmaster's primary responsibility is for his or her site.

Besides the division Webmasters, the company also has an Internet Services Group within its Information Technology section. This group includes a manager with extensive Web-based database experience, a programmer, and two programmers/content developers. They provide the programming and Intranet needs for the Web site to be interactive. They primarily work with the Webmasters to provide interactivity through databases.

"I am personally responsible for the service division," says Cooper. "It incorporates all of the company's support departments: human resources, accounting, community services, investor relations, travel, facilities, procurement, our company's training center, the information technology division, and the department I work in, which is called corporate communications."

Cooper joined the company before it opened its Intranet system. She helped gather all the information from the departments and developed Intranet sites

Meet Web Designers/Developers

for each of them. She reports to the vice president of corporate communications. She describes her duties, which are varied: "I meet with department contacts to continue developing their Web sites. I write HTML code for the sites. I work with graphic designers to develop the company's home page graphics for each department. I train department personnel to use Web conversion tools such as Word Internet Assistant to convert their own documents to HTML.

"I also create graphics for lower level Web pages. I attend monthly meetings with our company's Intranet Steering Committee to determine the efficiency of our internal Web page system. I also head a monthly Web developers group for the Internet Services Group and division Webmasters."

But that's not all. Cooper's other duties include keeping up-to-date on Web development technologies. She also works with an Internet Services Group to develop interactive databases on the Intranet. She works with a team to market the Intranet through promotional items. She writes technical users' guides and delivers presentations to visitors who want to learn about the company's Intranet system. Finally, she keeps all departments current on what they can do on the Intranet and how each department can work more efficiently and effectively.

"The method works well so far," says Cooper. "It allows division Webmasters to concentrate on developing their sites with up-to-date information and focus on making them user-friendly. It also allows the Internet Services Group to focus on the programming needs of the Intranet." The salary range for Cooper's work is from $50,000 to $80,000 a year.

Web Design for a Nonprofit Organization

Many public service organizations have Web sites. If you want a job as a Web designer that also helps you fulfill your desire to help other people, animals, the environment, or other causes, working for a public service organization can be especially rewarding. Gabriela Fitz, who is twenty-eight years old, designs the Web site for America's Second Harvest, a Chicago-based nonprofit organization devoted to helping Americans who are hungry. She holds a bachelor of arts degree in sociology from the University of California at Berkeley.

"After college, I did freelance Web projects," says Fitz. "They involved Web design, development, and production. After that, I became an editorial producer at *Cars.com*, a commercial Web site that sells new cars over the Internet."

Wanting a more personally satisfying job that involved social service, Fitz searched the Internet. "My interest lies with using the Web as a tool for social change," says Fitz. "I began looking for work more focused on noncommercial content. I learned about Second Harvest at a nonprofit Internet site called *Idealist.org*. I found a listing there for America's Second Harvest and landed the job I now have, planning and developing the organization's Web site. The job combines social issues with my Web design skills. I was no expert but knew enough about the work to bring my skills to the table, realizing there would be a lot for me to learn on the job."

Fitz's main responsibilities are to work on the organization's on-line communications strategy that brings hunger issues to Web users. "I create content for *Secondharvest.org* that gives people, policy makers, the media, and corporate donors information about hunger issues. The content I build for the site includes profiles of hungry Americans, profiles of food banks, statistics, fact sheets, and the latest news on the issue of hunger in America.

"Through the Web site, we want to give users information on hunger issues and easy access to tools for change. If you don't have a site that says anything, people won't see you as a source of information. People don't realize that hunger is such a huge issue in this country. I want people to leave the site having learned something and having the information they need to take action."

Fitz says the best thing about her job is it gives her the opportunity to use the Web as a creative tool for communicating information she considers important. She definitely enjoys her work because it utilizes her concern about social issues. Says Fitz, "I enjoy working on Web page content that matters."

Her advice to teenagers: "It's important to know the basics of HTML and Internet browser compatibility. When you have enough knowledge and experience designing Web sites, look on-line for jobs, including non-profit sites. If you're interested in helping others, search the Web for organizations that do public service work that interests you. Post your résumé on-line, and job opportunities will open up."

Fitz says the only thing about the job that isn't perfect for her is that "there aren't enough hours in the day to do all the outreach for an issue as big as hunger." While her work is personally satisfying, Fitz also earns a good salary. The salary range for her job is from $40,000 to $60,000 a year, plus employee health and other benefits.

A Web Designer's Career

Randy Ksar, who offered Web design job descriptions in the last chapter, tells about his career creating Web sites. "I started learning about the Internet in my senior year in high school in 1993-1994, when I had to choose between two classes: Art 2 or Internet," says Ksar. "Luckily, I chose Internet and learned to write HTML code, how to search the Internet, Web graphic design, and on-line chatting. Our teacher gave us direction and the ability to be creative and explore the Web."

While still in high school, Ksar first applied his Internet skills in a part-time internship at NASA-Ames Research Center in Moffett Field, California, the summer of 1993. "I was hired on to create and manage a Filemaker Pro database for their Flight Simulations Laboratory.

"This led to suggesting it would save money and paper to put their annual report and research papers on-line. My boss agreed, and I started scanning images and coding the documents. I learned the skills I needed by visiting other Web sites and reverse-engineering them. I spent many weekday and weekend hours viewing Web sites and testing HTML code and using Adobe PhotoShop to create graphics."

After high school, Ksar attended San Jose State University and graduated in 1999 with a bachelor of science degree in business administration with concentration in management information systems. "Throughout my college career, I had part-time jobs in one phase of computer work or another," says Ksar. "When my NASA internship ended, I got a consulting job building Web sites and tutoring other employees at Rasna Corporation, now owned by Parametric Technology. I

Meet Web Designers/Developers

was only seventeen when I landed my first Webmaster job. I was given a Powerbook and told to create a Web page. I wasn't given much direction, so I had to learn the technology and the process of building a corporate site."

Next, Ksar developed Intranet Web sites for various marketing divisions at Hewlett-Packard. From there he worked in the marketing communications department of Silicon Graphics. "The graphic designers in that group were some of the most creative people I've ever met in my life," says Ksar. "They taught me a lot about user interface design and color matching. Those skills really gave me a good eye for Web sites and distinguishing the ugly from the beautiful."

Ksar now works as an Internet engineer for Sony Electronics in California. "I am part of a three-person Web group," says Ksar. "I act as an Internet consultant to the product managers and help them showcase their products efficiently on the Web. Whether it involves coding and designing the site myself or hiring a freelance Web designer or developer, I take pride in my work and the responsibilities."

Ksar's career advice to young people: "In finding a Web design position, it's important to create an interesting résumé along with an on-line portfolio of Web pages you've worked on. If an employer views your Web site and doesn't see anything impressive within ten to fifteen seconds, it has given a bad impression. Your page has to have the Wow! factor.

"The most successful Web designers come from a print background, which means writing skills. Web designers generally have Adobe PhotoShop and Adobe Illustrator skills along with a knowledge of HTML and JavaScript. Now their coding skills are more utilized during the mock-up phase of Web site creation, so the actual programming gets handed over to the Web programmer/developer."

Ksar says finding a Web design job is fairly simple if the right steps are taken: "Just about every company has a Web presence today, and therefore has a Web team. If you're interested in working in a particular industry such as computers, surf on over to the top computing companies. Each of them lists job openings, including those for Web designers, on their Web sites. Then submit your résumé by e-mail and list one or more Web pages you've created."

Related Careers

Designing and maintaining sites on the Internet requires many specialized skills. Besides a Web designer or developer, there are other related careers. These include Webmaster, graphic artist, technical support representative, systems engineer, Internet applications programmer, Web consultant, multimedia developer, Web marketing director, and e-commerce manager.

As Web sites become more sophisticated and interactive, specialists may be needed to write the text and create the artwork for them. Every Web site that is created and maintained today may well be the work of a team of specialists.

Webmaster

Those who are responsible for all facets of a Web site and who may supervise one or more Web designers or developers or an entire team of site creators are called

Meet Web Designers/Developers

Webmasters. Web designers and developers often advance to the position of Webmaster.

Stephen Shoaff has been Webmaster for Nat Systems International in McLean, Virginia, since 1996. The company offers corporate, technical, and product information to the general public and provides technical and product support to customers. His responsibilities are both Internet and Intranet development, management, quality assurance, and usability issues for the company's Natstar application development technology.

Shoaff holds a bachelor's degree in computer science from George Mason University. His previous experience included Internet and Intranet consulting for another company where he helped develop Web sites and e-mail systems. He also conducted software process assessment and quality reviews.

"I report to the vice president of product development and other executives as specific Internet and Intranet needs require," says Shoaff. "A major current project I'm working on is to offer our Web site developers, sales staff, technical support, and customers customized views to product planning and data. Customers will be able to track problems from Web browsers and search for information on technical matters."

"The biggest job headache I have," says Shoaff, "is keeping up with the new technology. And I worry about a stale Web site that just doesn't attract viewers. Not finding enough qualified help, such as Web designers, keeps me from getting the job done."

Shoaff's workday is a typically full one for Webmasters. He says, "I arrive at my office at 6:30 AM, and spend quiet time working on new Web applications or page updates. Once the rest of the office gets in, I switch

Web site design requires artists to know about Web layout, graphics, and the value of blank space on a Web page.

to my more traditional software management role and get Web development in during the slower times. The day ends with a couple of evening hours devoted to Web page development. Most of my work on the Internet/Intranet stuff seems to get done at night."

Graphic Artist

With the growth of the Web, there is a growing need for artists who know how to translate their skills to electronic media. "The graphic design field is hot because of a variety of factors," says Christine Busby, communications director of the trade association American Center for Design in Chicago. "Because of the extensive use of graphics in Web design, the bar has been raised for electronic professionalism in graphics."

"Internet e-commerce and corporate Web sites have fueled the market for graphic designers," says Elizabeth Wells, creative recruiter at the Chicago placement agency, Artisans for Hire, Inc. "Demand outweighs supply. I can't fill about 30 percent of the Web graphic arts positions I have available."

The work requires artists with computer skills who know about Web layout, use of graphics, and also the value of blank space on a Web site. Graphic artists can generally pick and choose who to work for, and the trend is toward selecting a more casual, but highly creative workplace. "Everyone wants to work at a more creative shop or Internet start-up," says Karen Rasch, director of recruiting at Aquent Partners in Chicago. "Designers see themselves working at a start-up company located in a loft space with music playing. They see corporate Web departments almost as an oxymoron [an opposite or self-contradiction]."

To compete with more casual workplaces that appeal to artists and others attracted to Web design, many companies are offering higher pay, bonuses, and more benefits. One company offers to pay employees $1,500 a year toward advanced education related to their work.

Technical Support Representative

This job involves providing customer service to those accessing Web sites. Ellen Fielding, twenty-six, is a technical support representative at a major on-line entertainment catalog site. "Sometimes customers searching for a movie or CD at our Web site want to ask specific questions," says Fielding. "Or they may have trouble placing their on-line order. I assist them through e-mail or telephone calls."

The work requires a thorough knowledge of the company's Web site as well as people skills since there is direct contact with the consumer. Previous experience in customer relations and/or the Internet is helpful. Technical support representatives are hired both part-time and full-time, and working hours may be flexible. "It is an especially good part-time job for those going to college to learn more about developing Web sites," says Fielding. "That's how I started, and after a few years I had worked my way up to being a supervisor." Technical support representative salaries range from $20,000 to $30,000 a year.

Systems Engineer

Creating and maintaining Web sites involves the use of technical support machines and sophisticated software. It is the job of a systems engineer to be sure everything is in good working order. If you are more technically inclined, this might be a good Web design-related job for you.

C. J. Murzyn, twenty-eight, works as senior systems engineer at *Brittanica.com*, a Chicago-based provider of information products and services on the Internet. Before that, he was a systems administrator at the University of Illinois in Chicago from which he earned a bachelor of science degree in engineering. "I work on a team that is responsible for setting up and maintaining all the software, hardware, and networks that enable *Brittanica.com* to produce content," says Murzyn. "I put the operating systems in place so that viewers can search the site for information, including

Meet Web Designers/Developers

the full text of our *Encyclopedia Brittanica*, as well as our books and more than seventy magazines."

The technology Murzyn sets up and maintains includes databases, search functions, and software applications. He also ensures the system's security, so no one can alter or destroy information on the site. When new content is to be added to the site, he makes sure the technology is in place for it. "The best thing about my job," says Murzyn, "is that I get to learn about and work with the equipment that continually improves the Web site." His advice to young people: "There aren't enough systems engineers out there. It's a wide-open job market. Learn everything you can about computers and Web design. Read trade magazines and keep playing with the technical toys." The salary range for systems engineers is $62,000 to $94,000.

Web Consultant

After gaining several years' experience as a Web designer, you could become a Web consultant. Your job might not be to develop a good Web site for a client, but to undo the bad work of a previously designed Internet site. An example of this type of problem was reported in *CIO Web Business* magazine.

A leading consumer health magazine published in Westport, Connecticut, hired a well-known Web design firm in New York City to build its Web site. The work was to take six months and cost $345,000. A year later the site was still not finished and the cost was already at $240,000. The design firm said the site could be completed for an additional $219,000. The magazine had no alternative but to keep going and keep paying.

Web consultants come to the rescue in situations like this magazine publisher found himself in. "Most problems arise when a company hires a firm to start building a site and then realizes halfway through its completion that it's not what the company wanted," says Rosalind Resnick, president of Net Creations, a New York City Internet marketing firm.

A Web consultant is to the Internet what a script doctor is to the movies. He or she is an expert at changing what someone else has not done satisfactorily. The improvements require extensive knowledge of problem-solving that only comes with years of experience developing and maintaining effective Web sites. The pay is often very good, ranging into the tens of thousands of dollars per job.

Multimedia Developer

Many Web sites incorporate multimedia features such as videos and sound. These high-tech features require special skills. Lynn Ramsay, thirty, is a multimedia developer at Access Technology, a Chicago-based company. After earning a bachelor of science degree in business from Eastern Illinois University, she got her multimedia developer job at Access Technology through an employment recruiter.

"I took the job because it was a good opportunity and I liked the people at Access," says Ramsay. "My main responsibility is programming multimedia presentations for interactive video kiosks. [Kiosks feature advertising or

Meet Web Designers/Developers

promotion programs viewed on a computer monitor.] Clients ranging from pharmaceutical companies to those selling athletic equipment use kiosks for trade shows or as information tools so people can learn about a product."

Web developers meet with clients to learn what they want their pages to accomplish and look like, and kiosk developers learn what type of presentations the clients want. Ramsay works with a development team that decides on a kiosk program design. "I take the elements of the design and blend them into a software package that will be installed into the kiosk," says Ramsay. She does this by using software such as Macromedia Director and Visual Basic to blend audio, video, and graphics into the package. Ramsay suggests that young people interested in a career as a multimedia director learn different technologies and have versatile skills such as HTML and Java.

Web Marketing Director

Rick Brennan's work as Web marketing director at one of the giants in the information technology industry, Sun Microsystems, Inc., is typical of this Web-related career. Brennan holds a bachelor's degree in biomedical and electrical engineering from Duke University and is working toward a master's in business administration.

Brennan's work at Sun Microsystems involves working with others on complementary how-to pages that detail how the company's Web pages are developed. He also manages its Intranet offerings so they can be moved to the Internet and used in conjunction with other companies. "Currently, I'm also working with others to develop the company's global networks," says Brennan. "A future project is to develop the company's highly interactive Web applications."

Brennan says his biggest job headache is the fast pace of changing technology: "Many people are threatened by technology. It's a human trait. It's challenging to change this fast." He worries about tight deadlines: "I'm constantly asked, 'Can you get the resources? Can you make things as fast as you promise them?' Some of the harder things still take planning and development time. You can't solve problems in Internet time."

Brennan's typical workday consists of working with outside Web developers, supporting internal systems, and fielding customer requests for products and services. "A year and a half ago, there wasn't anyone to call for this information. Now, there are too many people giving answers. It's a challenge to evaluate the potential products, offerings, and people involved in Web development."

Brennan talks about the biggest change in his job and in the profession itself in the past year: "Technology will touch everyone in the world. You couldn't have convinced me of that just two years ago."

E-Commerce Manager

A strong knowledge of developing and expanding the interactive features of Web sites is essential to the work of an e-commerce manager. E-commerce is the relatively new and enormously fast-growing business of selling and buying electronically over the Internet.

Meet Web Designers/Developers

For the past three years, Peter J. Jacobs has been manager of e-commerce for the 3M Corporation, headquartered in St. Paul, Minnesota. He holds a bachelor's degree in mathematics and psychology and master's degrees in both statistics and marketing. Jacobs is chairperson of 3M's e-commerce business team, overseeing its e-commerce consulting service and managing both Internet and Intranet development for the company.

"There is no typical day at my job," says Jacobs. "Every day is fast-paced, requiring me to operate on three levels. Strategic, for thinking and planning. Tactical, for building things. And operational, for keeping it all running. It's interesting, trying to do all three at once."

Jacobs's current projects are to use the Web to extend the company's marketing reach and to deliver improved customer service on its Web site. His future goal is to use the Web as a window to a variety of information for 3M and its customers.

"I prefer to view my biggest job headaches in terms of challenges," says Jacobs. "First, working across a variety of 3M functions and external organizations to develop e-commerce solutions. Second, ensuring that e-commerce and electronic marketplace activities are business-driven, not technology-driven.

"I am concerned about how to apply these new, very exciting capabilities so that we provide business value. In the first phases of Web activities, many folks talked about the need for super-attractive sites to pull people in. Now we're focusing more on business value."

Like others in the information technology field whose work is related to Web development, Jacobs says the biggest change he has seen in his job and

Careers in Web Design

profession in the past year is the increased pace of the Web. "There is a greater than ever expectation for Web site reliability twenty-four hours a day, seven days a week."

From these reports on Web-related and often Web-dependent professions, it becomes obvious that the work requires specialized knowledge and experience. The work also requires an eagerness to be a part of the information technology world, a willingness to work hard, and the ability to keep up with fast changes in each field.

The Making of a Web Site

6

A site on the Web is a combination of text and graphics that may be on one page or contain links to others. More sophisticated Web sites contain audio and/or video features, and some allow users to interact by way of chat groups, on-line forums, and e-mail or fax communication. How do you get all that together? Whole books are written on how to design a Web site, but this chapter hopes to keep it short and simple.

What's on a Web Page

There are three basic elements that go into a Web page: text, design, and programming. Each element is important to the success of a site and requires special skills. One person may have one or more of the skills, but often it takes a team of people to cover all of the skills necessary to develop a really good Web site.

— Writing. One person, or a team of writers, may create the content for a Web site. Information on the site must be clearly written, covering everything that is supposed to be discussed.

— Design. The design of a Web site is its shape or style. Design requires artistic skills in balancing the text and graphics. The size and font of text and headlines can add artistic touches to a Web site, as can the placement of graphics and background for the page.

— Programming. Programming means a set of instructions entered into a computer to tell it how to do something. Instructions are written in computer languages such as Java.

Most people have at least some writing or design abilities they can use in developing Web sites. Computer programming is a skill that has to be learned. The best Web designers learn computer programming, HTML, and Web design software.

Creating a Site

When creating any kind of Web site, it's helpful to sit down with pen and paper and write one sentence about your site's purpose. Will it be a personal Web site about a hobby or a site related to business?

Just for an example, let's say your Web site will be a fan site about your favorite rock group. For the purpose of this sample exercise, let's call them the Alley Cats from Mars. When the time comes, we'll name your page *Alleycatsfrommars.com*.

The Making of a Web Site

First, go on-line and run a search to see if any Web site already exists on the rock group (chances are there will be several). You can still create your own, but you can get ideas from existing sites on that group. Before starting to build your Web site, decide what it will look like and who its potential visitors will be. In the case of a fan site, that's easy. Other fans of your favorite rock group will be your intended visitors. If you were building a Web site for an automobile dealer, people looking to buy the cars sold at the dealership would be your site's target audience.

Now decide how your site will tell about the rock group. A short index is a good way to summarize what your site will contain. You might divide your site into the lives and careers of each member of the rock group before they got together. Then tell about the rock group's beginning, its rise to fame, and its present success. Make a list of what will go into each phase, in both text and photos.

Create a Site Plan

Now that you have a list of what your rock group site will contain, draw up a simple diagram—a site design plan based upon that list. That will look like a family tree diagram. The top square is your Web site's home page with the index and photo of each performer in the rock group, and maybe even one of yourself. The squares below will be links to other pages that contain information and photos of each of the rock performer's life and career.

Make an Inventory List

Next, make a list of information and graphics you will want to put in the links on your site. Keep track of all this by labeling a manila folder for each link and putting articles and photos pertaining to each link in each folder.

Design a Page Grid

If you were making a magazine about your favorite rock group, you would design the first page on a sheet of paper. Do the same to design the home page of your Web site. *Alleycatsfrommars.com*'s home page would have a headline identifying it, your name and e-mail address, and space for some text and photos. Remember to keep it simple. The grid is just to guide you in what each page of your Web site will look like. Next, create page grids for each link to other pages about your rock group.

Content and Code

Type the content for your site's home page and all link pages. Decide what font and size you will use for headlines, subheads, and body text. You can use HTML (hypertext markup language), which is a code for Web pages, or use any of several templates that are built into most word-processing programs, such as Microsoft Word or Appleworks. Templates are pre-formatted Web pages. Places for text and graphics are already designed into the template or sample Web page. You just add the text and photos where the template suggests. Many new Web page designers use Freeway 1.02, a good graphical Web editor.

Store all the text in your computer as plain text files (like NotePad or WordPad), which will be added later to your Web site. Software called HTML Markup 3.0 processes text files to help with this. Jean Kaiser, host of

Create an inventory list of the links that you want on your site.

the Web design site for *About.com*, suggests, "After you are familiar with HTML, you will probably want to start using an editor. Without a doubt, it makes life easier."

Store the Graphics

You will need to use a scanner to transfer photos of your rock performers onto your Web site. Scan each photo and store them as either a JPEG or GIF. Experiment to see which of the two formats you prefer to use. After, you could manipulate the photos using programs such as Adobe PhotoShop or Illustrator. Photo manipulation programs allow you to do many things, including cropping and changing the size of a photo, its color, and its density (how light or dark it is). Organize all graphics into a folder. This will be the home graphics directory for all the photos and any artwork on your Web site. Now you can add the text and graphics to the template pages. After this is done, study and edit each page carefully to be sure you have everything where you want it. Make any necessary adjustments.

Get Your Site Seen!

With over a billion Web sites already on-line and thousands being added each day, there is strong competition for good domain names (the addresses of Web sites). It's a good idea to register your Web site even before you build it.

Registering a Web Site

Register *alleycatsfrommars.com* through any of several services such as Register.com (*www.register.com*) or

The Making of a Web Site

Network Solutions (*www.networksolutions.com*). Your site will be given a URL (Universal Resource Locator). Your Web site's URL, *www.alleycatsfrommars.com*, becomes its address on the World Wide Web.

Domain name registration services usually cost money and must be paid for by credit card. However, you can register your site for free through most Internet Service Providers (ISPs), such as Prodigy or America OnLine, or through sites like gURL.com (*www.gurl.com*). Once you register your name and interests through the site, you are given a space through their server. For example, if you used gURL.com, your URL might be *www.gurlpages.com/music/alleycatsfrommars*.

Put Your Site On-line

Next, upload the site. Do this by logging on to your Web server with an FTP client such as Anarchy. Then upload your Web site to the directory where Web sites are located. After your Web site is on-line, check it out. Type its URL and add "test.html" to the end of it so it reads *www.alleycatsfrommars.com/test.html*. Your Web site about your favorite rock group should appear on your computer monitor. Proofread each page of your Web site and correct any errors, then get the corrections on-line.

Spread the Word

Let the world know about your Alley Cats from Mars Web site by registering it with various search engines. Get help in this by going to Webmaster Station at *www.exeat.com/metatags/meta.shtml*. Then go to Webmaster Station's URL submission page at *www.exeat.com/submit/submit.shtml.* This enables you to submit your Web site to any of eighteen search engines.

Need Help?

Designing a Web site is no easy task. The good news is that there is plenty of help out there, much of it free. Many Internet search sites, such as Yahoo!, Infoseek, and Netscape, offer free instruction on how to design a site. For more information, check out these sites:

About.com
www.webdesign.about.com
Comprehensive site that includes links and free text code.

Builder.com
www.builder.com
Advice and helpful downloads on building Web sites.

HTML Writers Guild
www.hwg.org
Free reference material and on-line instruction.

Wacky HTML
www.webdevelopersjournal.com/wacky
Information on adding fun things like wiggling type, color fades, and other pizzazz to a Web site.

Webmaster Station
www.exeat.com
Information and tools for getting Web sites on-line.

Webmonkey
www.webmonkey.com
Design collective that offers information on software, including JavaScript, HTML, and Photoshop.

Programming Your Site

Nearly every site on the Web relies upon HTML to define its appearance. HTML editors and templates, which are ready-made formats of Web pages, can be helpful in designing your Web site. Elements of templates also can be useful for more experienced site designers. However, most professional Web designers suggest that novices learn a little HTML before using templates.

HTML is the most commonly used code for designing Web sites and is considered to be the lifeblood of the Web. HTML defines areas of text by "tagging" them. Tags are like a shorthand of symbols for page design.

HTML Tags

Angle brackets ("<" and ">") define HTML tags for the computer. Every HTML command starts with a beginning tag that indicates the element type. They begin with the open angle bracket and end with the close angle bracket. Between the two brackets are the instructions for the Web page.

Ending tags start with an open angle bracket that is followed by a forward slash (</). They end with a close angle bracket(>). This tells the computer where the action or element ends. The close tag for an HTML ele-

Basic Tags

<HTML></HTML>
Identifies a file as an HTML document.

<HEAD></HEAD>
Contains information not displayed on the page.

</META>
Allows you to use keywords or a brief description to make your page come up in search engines.

<TITLE></TITLE>
Contains information displayed in the title bar at the top of the browser window.

<BODY> </BODY>
Contains everything on the page.

<FONT></FONT>
Allows you to alter the font of a section of text.

<B></B>
Bold text.

<I></I>
Italic text.

<U></U>
Underlined text.

<TABLE></TABLE>
Creates a table, such as those used in financial Web sites.

ment </html>, for example, indicates the end of an HTML document.

Text Editors and Scripters

Text Editors
Many Web designers find their work goes faster and easier using an HTML text editor. The following text editors, listed alphabetically, are good for both beginners and more advanced Web designers.

Aardvark Pro 3.0.1
> *www.ntmg.net/aardvark*
> For Windows computers. HTML is produced by typing directly or activated by toolbar buttons, aided by drag-and-drop technology. It includes a useful Text Spell Checker and there is a viewer for checking the appearance of the active HTML file window.

Allaire HomeSite 4.0
> *www.allaire.com/products/homesite*
> For Windows computers. Good for beginners because of its interactive design of HTML structures such as lists, tables, and frame sets. Design-mode editing lets you edit a page the way it will look on a browser.

BBEdit 5.1.1
> *www.barebones.com/products/bbedit*
> CD software for Macintosh computers. BBEdit

is the most popular HTML text editor for Mac users. It is based on a main text edit screen with a separate toolbar window. Most toolbar buttons, form fields, or menu items create a single HTML tag. Special features include drag and drop, viewer, text formatter, link checker, and scripting tool.

Sausage Software HotDog Professional 5.5

www.sausage.com/software
For Windows computers. For the beginner, there are help windows bracketing a file being worked on. It also has a viewer for checking the page's appearance. For the more advanced, features include ways to maximize image presentation and a large clipboard for code transfer between pages.

SoftQuad HoTMetal Pro 6.0

www.sq.com/products/hotmetal
For Windows computers. This editor has a "resource manager" from which images, code blocks, or other items can be dragged and dropped in the Web page.

W3C Amaya

www.w3.org/amaya
For Windows computers. A good HTML editor for the beginner. It offers simultaneous browsing and editing, math markup language, and tag nesting views.

Scripters

The most exciting and effective Web sites contain interactive features so users can communicate with site hosts. Interactivity requires more than HTML skills. For successful interactive page elements, Web designers utilize scripts. Scripts are small programs embedded in a Web site's HTML structure. They tell a browser how to act in response to input from the page's user.

HTML was designed as a graphical markup Web design language. It tells a browser how page elements look. Scripts, on the other hand, tell a browser how to act. Scripts and HTML work together. Each gives a browser specialized information, but scripts give Web site visitors more interactivity. Just as there is software to help you learn HTML, there is other software to learn scripting. Some further information on them can be found at these Web sites:

Cut-N-Paste JavaScript

www.infohiway.com/javascript/index.htm
Speeds scripting by letting you cut and paste the text of hundreds of scripts for your own needs. It includes a variety of animation, calendars, clocks, guestbooks, games, and security features. A special feature is its section called Top 10 Scripts.

JavaScript Source

javascript.internet.com
Besides offering hundreds of ready-made JavaScripts, this site lists the ten newest scripts in a pull-down menu. There also is a JavaScript newsletter to answer questions and offer support.

> **ScriptSearch JavaScript**
> *www.scriptsearch.com/pages/4.shtml*
> A directory links to more than 1,000 scripts from independent sources where you can learn more about scripting for Web interactivity.

Test Your Web Site

Before posting your site on the Internet, test it to see how well it does what you want it to. Proofread the site for errors or ways to improve it. After you are satisfied that your site is the best it can be, ask friends to navigate it. They may find mistakes you didn't, or suggest ways to make your site more effective or easier to navigate. Other points of view can help you get it right.

"Building an easy-to-use Web site takes time, experience, and many forehead-slapping lessons you wish you didn't have to learn," says Lisa Schmeiser, a Web site developer for Studio Verso in San Francisco. "Fortunately, if you learn from the past mistakes of Web pioneers, you'll have a strong beginning for making your site a more user-friendly place to visit."

Web Design Tips

The look of a Web site is usually the first thing visitors notice. It often influences whether they stay and read it or move on to another site. If the site is too cluttered, the viewer may become impatient in trying to figure it out and leave the site. Following are some tips on effective Web design from both designers and clients for whom they designed the pages.

Importance of Planning

Most Web designers agree that the importance of a successful Web site is that it does what it's intended to do: attract viewers and, in the case of selling a product or service, create a sale. That means a comprehensive Web page plan.

"The argument that 'just being there' is reason enough to be on the Web sounds more specious every day," says Webmaster consultant Matthew Cutler, president of the Webmasters Guild, the nation's first professional organization for Webmasters. The guild (*www.webmaster.org*) is a nonprofit organization dedicated to educating, promoting, and unifying the global Webmaster community. Cutler is also founder and director of business development at Net.GenesisCorp., a provider of Web performance and usage analysis software (*www.netgen.com*).

"What with promotional sites clocking in at several hundred thousand dollars and transactional sites generally reaching into the millions, companies would be foolish to venture on-line without a clear idea of what they want to achieve and how they want to achieve it. So it's not unusual that the ranks of the motivationless sites are getting thinner," Cutler says. "Yes, some companies still err by launching Web sites that have no objective other than giving the chief operating officer something to talk about at cocktail parties. But as Web functionality becomes increasingly diverse, more companies are making the opposite mistake: trying to do too many things at once. As a result, they are doing few things well."

Cutler says companies need a business plan aimed at making the Web effective for them and keeping it manageable. He suggests that the person in a company responsible for creating that plan is a business strategist who works as part of the Webmaster's team.

"The business strategist defines and then prioritizes an organization's Internet goals based on their importance to the corporate mission," Cutler explains. "Within the Webmaster team, the business strategist must weigh the cases put forth by various [officers of the company] and then select the prime objectives of the company's site."

Cutler suggests that at first, there be a single overall objective for the company's Web site. This helps to maintain focus during the critical formulative stages of the site's life cycle. If this is not realistic for the site, then no more than three key objectives should be decided upon, and the priority of each clearly defined.

"This is not a simple process," Cutler admits. "The Web offers such juicy opportunities to so many people that numerous groups [within a company], from human resources to technical support to sales and marketing, are likely to compete for on-line primacy. The business strategist must choose among them by evaluating factors such as competitive pressures, internal demand, and, of course, the all-important expected [financial] return on investment."

Once the company's Web site is on-line and doing business, it is important to constantly evaluate how effective it is in carrying out the original site plan. "Because of the rapid evolution of the Internet," says Cutler, "the maintenance phase is likely to be at least as time consuming as initial planning efforts."

Be Consistent

Keep your site's layout consistent. Each page should be designed about the same so they all have a similar look.

Designing each page differently can be confusing to the viewer. Uniformity of layout can be achieved by repeating a logo—a name, symbol, or graphic that identifies your page. Or use the same font style and type size for each page, as well as the same color background.

Make Navigation Easy

Create a good navigation plan for viewers of your Web site. Make it easy and logical for viewers to move from page to page within the site by way of hyperlinks, graphics bars, or buttons. Put the navigation menu for your site on the home page, then repeat it in the same place throughout the site. That way, a visitor knows where to find it as he or she moves from page to page or link to link.

A typical example of a navigation menu such as the following could appear at the top or bottom of personal Web pages:

Home/Photos/Résumé/Hobbies

The HTML code for the menu looks like this:

```
<CENTER>
<A HREF="index.html">Home</A> |
<A HREF="photos.html">Photos</A> |
<A HREF="resume.html">Résumé</A> |
<A HREF="hobbies.html">Hobbies</A> |
</CENTER>
```

The vertical character separating each link is known as a pipe. It is found to the right of the key for closing brackets on the computer keyboard.

Viewers of your Web site will look for a starting point and easy access to the contents of the site. Don't confuse viewers by letting them wonder how to get out of a link and back to the Web site's home page. Be sure to clearly place a Return To Home Page sign at the end of each page.

Choose Pleasing Colors

Web sites with colors that are too bright or that do not blend well together on a page can make it hard to read or just displeasing. When tempted to use a color background for a Web page, consider if it may be distracting. In general, avoid bright colors for a background and just use plain white as a color. Color is recommended, however, as background for tables, to set them apart from the page's text. The entire table can be colored or just parts of it, such as every other row. Avoid "nesting" tables. It can be confusing for viewers if they are asked to read tables within tables within tables.

Design Tips On-Line

More tips on effective Web design can be found on-line. In addition to the previous sites listed on building a Web site, these additional sites offer suggestions in how to improve them:

Dimitry's Design Lab

www.webreference.com/dlab

Lynda Weinman

www.lynda.com

Yale Style Manual
www.info.med.yale.edu/caim/manual

Avoid These Mistakes

It's not enough to know how to design an effective Web site. You have to know what mistakes to avoid. Monique Harris, creator of the Web Hosting and Designers Marketing Base, says there are six main mistakes Web site designers make in selling themselves and their skills to prospective employers.

"There are over ten thousand Web site designers and developers listed on Yahoo! alone," says Harris. "Competition is indeed thick. But you can literally zoom past at least 80 percent of your competitors if you know how to capitalize on their mistakes."

The six most common mistakes that are found in the sample Web pages that designers show potential clients, and how to avoid them, are as follows:

1. Designers don't check their own sites for proper grammar and correct spelling. Avoid this by running your site through both a grammar and spell checker. Then give it to an editor for further polishing.

2. Designers often use cheap or over-familiar graphics on their Web site. Instead, use some of the better clip art programs such as ArtToday, Gini's Connoisseur Collection, Clip-Art.com, and Barry's Clip Art Collection. Better yet, learn to create your own original graphics.

Make sure that you talk to your clients in a way that they will understand—try not to be too technical.

3. Web sites take too long to load. Viewers get impatient if a Web site takes more than ten or fifteen seconds to appear on their monitor. Re-evaluate the speed of access of your Web site so that its home page and all link pages come up as fast as possible.

4. Viewers don't know where to find your Web site. Register your domain with a service such as Internic. It will cost about $20 a month or less, but Web surfers will be able to find your site.

5. There's no clue as to what your fee is. When marketing your Web design services, be sure to add information not only about what kind of sites you can create but what you charge. The range is wide, according to what services are provided. Complete site design fees can be from a few hundred to several thousand dollars, depending on the complexity of the job and the time required to complete it.

6. Site developers talk over the client's technical head. Do not use cool techie terms to motivate the prospective client, such as saying you use Java, JavaScript, Perl, Cold Fusion, and DHTML to build a Web site. The client may not understand a word you're saying and feel you're conning him or her. It's okay to say what technology you'll use to create a Web site, but be sure to explain what it will do for the page.

Importance of Web Design Skills

Surf the Web and you may find some on-line chat groups in heated debate over the work of Web designers and developers. During the writing of this book, a very lively debate was in full swing on one Internet site. Half a dozen Web site creators were holding forth on the subject of what skills are really essential in getting a job as a Web designer and/or developer and the work in general. Following are highlights of their on-line debate.

> *Helen: "I just got back from a job interview for a Web designer position. I was a little disappointed to find they were looking for someone with more computer programming skills, such as Visual Basic, asp., C++, along with the HTML and DreamWeaver skills.*
>
> *"I can design a Web page through a WYSIWYG (What You See Is What You Get) program as well as hand coding, but I do not have an interest in learning a programming language. Is this something that I need to know to get a job designing Web sites?*

Careers in Web Design

"I like the design, layout, and creative aspects of Web design and thought I had the skills to do the job. Until today, that is. It was very frustrating to find out that programming skills are what they were looking for. What kind of additional skills do I need to make it as a Web designer?"

Bill: *"There are many aspects to Web development, many specialties. You could learn Java really well, or Flash, for interactive content design. You could study databases and become a competent programmer. You could concentrate solely on Internet marketing and ad banner business. Or you could just do consulting.*

"There are many fields within 'Web designer,' and employers will often look for the jack-of-all-trades. But there are many niches for specialists, so choose what you really want to do and stick with it!"

Chris: *"Let's clearly draw the line of distinction between what is a 'Web designer' and what is a 'Web developer' because there is a huge difference.*

"You could specialize in graphics and custom art, even photography. This would be the province of a Web designer, not a developer. At my Web design firm, we don't want our developers to even try their hand at graphics or photo manipulation.

"Yes, you could learn Java or Flash, but Java [is more important] for the developer,

The Making of a Web Site

and Flash [is more important] for the designer. Java, even for an experienced programmer, is a very advanced programming language. A few years ago, Web developers were using it to make animations and create interactivity, but not anymore. JavaScript and Flash have taken that over. But no serious interactive shop is going to expect their Web designer to know Java.

"Studying databases and becoming a programmer are jobs for Web developers, not for designers. As for Web marketing and the ad banner business, Web advertising has become a billion dollar industry. Web marketing is another position altogether and requires extensive knowledge of media, media rates, and media contacts. A few years ago, it was possible to fake yourself as an Internet marketer. Nowadays, if you don't have a marketing background and a serious knowledge of the industry, you'll be exposed fairly quickly.

"The Web has become too complicated for someone to sell himself or herself as a jack-of-all-trades. While it is very important for a designer to know HTML and some JavaScript, as well as being aware of other Web technologies, there is a world of difference between Web design and Web development."

Jamie: "I go by both designer and developer. In this meat-grinder world, Web developers such as programmers, database managers, etc., are forced to pick up things they don't normally do, such as photography and graphic design. This cross-training produces better professionals and more independent Web developers. In my company, if you don't know it all, you don't get hired.

"Java for the designer? Flash for the developer? Either of these skills can be learned by each independent profession. There is no need to force one profession to learn one or the other. To create a competent Web page, both skills are needed. Also, the company I design for requires Web designers to know Java.

"I don't have a marketing background, but I have pulled in over a million hits to a client's Web site. Everyone knows I don't have a background in marketing and advertising, but when you can pull a million hits, you really don't need it.

"Today's competitive edge requires Web professionals who know and do all. My company's smaller teams of Web developers can push through entire multimillion dollar contracts in less than a year. Three people to design, develop, and implement sophisticated e-commerce solutions, complete with professional design and custom programming and interactive content.

"Our company's president understood the Internet back in 1992 and saw the need for highly trained, highly adaptable Web site developers/designers. We are not either. We are both.

"The differences are perhaps wide in the Web community. But to experienced *professionals, there is not much of a difference. It all comes down to a matter of what you can do."*

Chris: *"I both agree and disagree with you, Jamie. While it's true that it's necessary to know a lot more than just what you do when working in the Internet industry, it's also true that one must do one thing extremely well!*

"It's no longer acceptable for a programmer to buy clip art CDs and call himself or herself a designer. Sure, it's best if the programmer understands design, but the designers at my firm are all extremely highly trained and great at what we do. Likewise, we wouldn't look at a designer who just bought a Java book and thinks he or she can do both. Our developers are masters at it. We call on them to write customized, Web-based applications for our clients.

"Sure, a Web designer could spend time and learn Java. But I prefer that my designers learn Flash and learn how to work with the developer to create dynamically generated artwork and custom interactive content for our clients.

"I do think that my understanding of marketing, technology, programming, strategy, and communication has made me a better Web designer. It has all helped me to create projects that bring tremendous value to our clients. But I am not a believer of being a jack-of-all-trades and a master of none. These days on the Web, you'd better be master of something!

Careers in Web Design

"Web building is like basketball. Everyone can dribble, shoot, pass, and play defensively. But everyone has roles, and the team can win only if people know those roles and do them well. Otherwise, you're stuck with the rampant mediocrity that is all too common on the Web. Too many people do a lot of things, just none of them well."

Jamie: "I agree with you in many aspects. I just wanted to tell Helen to pick something she liked. Whether it be design or development, work and learn it. Whether it be photography or Web-based application design, keep learning. The important thing is to first be a master at your given specialty. Then learn other things.

"As someone who hires Web designers, my final advice to you, Helen, is make sure you're a [great] designer, first and foremost. Excel at that. Create compelling, interactive experiences for users and your clients. That's what most interactive Web shops need from their designers and what is sorely missing on the Web. No one will punish you if you can't write a Java applet! One day, Helen, you could be a superstar Web creator yourself."

Helen: "Wow! Look at what I started with my little question! But thanks, guys. I learned a lot! Now which one of you is going to hire me?"

Looking to the Future

Just before the close of the last millennium, eight top American business executives were asked to choose the most important developments of the twentieth century. High on their lists were the airplane, television, computer, and the Internet. "Before this century, science did not matter to the average person," said Franklin D. Raines, chairman of Fannie Mae, the world's largest non-bank financial services company. "In this century, science is changing our lives fundamentally."

The Internet Century

Stephen M. Case, chairman and chief executive of America Online, one of the major providers of access to the Web, agrees. "I do think the next century is going to be the Internet century," he said. "The Internet has the ability to transform all aspects of what we do to gather information, shop, communicate, or be entertained. It is very, very empowering."

In the next century, the Internet will transform how people gather information, shop, and communicate.

An important part of the Internet's future and impact on commerce and society will be the continued expansion of the Web. That translates to a secure future in career opportunities for those who design and maintain sites on the Web. Knowledge and experience in Web design will continue to be the tools for success in Web development careers. The challenge will be to keep up with the ever advancing technology.

A decade ago, the job of creating Web sites was an unknown occupation in which one technologically-savvy individual could design a site. According to the Webmaster's Guild, the job has now become highly sophisticated and requires the skills of a multidisciplinary team. During this short period of growth, Web server technology has advanced from delivering simple text to Web sites that contain all types of multimedia. One of the newest Web technologies, HTTP/1.1, provides a means for the Web to be truly "worldwide" by adding various languages to Web sites.

This is especially important as e-commerce continues to expand on a global scale. Web sites with foreign language translation capabilities are not only increasingly important for major companies doing business between cities such as New York and Tokyo or Paris, but for small businesses anywhere.

For example, an Inuit community in a remote Alaskan village sells hand-carved Eskimo art to collectors all over the world by means of their Web site, which local high school students learned how to design. Their site's ability to communicate in a number of languages makes it possible for the village to sell to customers in ten different counties. According to the Webmaster's Guild, Webmasters will start including internationalization, translation, and language experts as part of present and future corporate Web design teams.

A Bright Future

There are more than a billion Web sites on the Internet. This is a remarkable number considering that just a decade ago, only a few thousand existed in scientific and high-tech circles. More than $19 billion a year is spent on business Web site development. Advances in information and Web technology are making it possible for sites to do more, especially in interactive features and wireless computers. Web designers and developers can expect ongoing work into the new millennium.

Proof of a bright future in Web design can be found every day in the business or technology sections of newspapers and magazines. As the Internet continues to expand and thousands of additional Web sites launch every day, there is little doubt that the future for Web site designers is assured.

Web Domain Names

Page one of the *Wall Street Journal*'s Marketplace section read, "For the Keeper of Web Names, a $17 Billion Deal." The article reported that VeriSign, a leader in authentication technology based in Mountain View, California, had negotiated a multibillion dollar stock transaction to buy into Network Solutions, Inc., the chief registrar of Internet domain (Web page) names.

By that date, Network Solutions had already dispensed some nine million Internet addresses to customers around the world. VeriSign made the offer anticipating that millions more companies would need domain names for their new sites once they are developed. "We think there are almost 160 million businesses or organizations that could need a Web identity," said Stratton Sclavos, VeriSign's chief executive officer. Each of those estimated 160 million new Web sites will have to be designed. Will you be one of the designers?

New Developments Mean Exciting Opportunities

Digital Technology

Recently-introduced digital cameras, which create superior pictures, and digital camcorders that create both higher quality video and added sound, immediately began to be used in Web sites for commercial and individual purposes. Another aspect of the digital revolution's effect on Web technology could be seen when Simon & Schuster publishers gave a major boost to the

Looking to the Future

fledgling world of on-line books. It released a short story by the champion horror author Stephen King in digital format only. "Riding the Bullet," a new sixty-six-page ghost story by the genre's leading author, would not be available in traditional printed book form, but could be read only on computer screens. Fans of King would pay $2.50 to on-line booksellers such as *Amazon.com* in order to read the book on their computer monitors. "We are rooting for the electronic form of book publishing to work," said Jack Romanos, president and chief operating officer of Simon and Schuster. "This has the potential to redefine mass market bookselling for us."

On-line editions of new books means potential growth for the book publishing business. It also means more work for Web designers who will be assigned to develop and/or maintain the Internet sites for the publishers of on-line books and on-line sellers of those books.

Voice Mail over the Internet

Another example of how new technology is incorporated into use of the Internet, bringing with it more work for Web page designers, was the trend toward use of voice mail over the Internet. Voice mail is available to anyone willing to listen to advertising spots over the telephone. A system called Echobuzz, aimed at teenagers, is a potential market for teens who want to leave messages that can't be heard by Mom or Dad.

Teens fill out forms at *www.echobuzz.com* asking for contact information and details about their interests, such as favorite music, sports, and hobbies. After signing up for Echobuzz, they receive e-mail messages containing personal identification numbers that give them access to their accounts. The system was designed by Blue Diamond Software of Irvine, California to earn revenue from advertisers. It also was developed as a way to test the company's speech-recognition software, according to the company's president, Blaine Ung.

The Wireless Web

Computer technology changes almost as fast as the weather. Each day, not only new types of computers but new versions of software are being developed that may well change every facet of what we know today about computers. In just the next five years, more new developments and entirely new concepts in information technology may make today's high-tech world as obsolete as the horse and buggy. They are likely to have profound effects on how Web sites are designed and what they will be capable of containing or doing, including more expansive interactive, sound, and new three-dimensional features.

One of the new technologies with especially exciting applications to the Internet is "the wireless Web." Major telecommunications firms offer wireless Web service by way of cellular telephones that can access the Internet. It's an exciting technology, but at this date, only text can be retrieved by the wireless Web, not graphics. Also, only a limited number of Web sites can be accessed, mainly those where the telephone service provider, such as Sprint, has digital coverage.

However, the wireless Web does have a potentially exciting future. With further advances in the technology, consumers could hop from Web site to Web site with their cellular phones as easily as they can from their home or work computers.

Looking to the Future

The wireless revolution got a big boost early in 2000 when a group of former executives from the Microsoft Corporation announced they were investing in new companies developing wireless Internet access.

"We believe that the next big thing that is going to change the world, as the PC [personal computer] and the Internet did, will be wireless Internet," said Brad Silverberg, who guided Microsoft into the Internet age. "It's going to be one of those tidal waves in technology."

Consumers are accessing the Internet from handheld computers or cellular phones in rapidly increasing numbers. Computer industry analysts say that companies with Web sites need to consider whether they want to take their sites wireless. It is predicted that wireless Web activity will deliver data at speeds at least ten times what today's wireless phones achieve. Wireless Web technology will be especially useful in making hand-held electronic products such as cellular phones and computers easier to use, particularly in e-commerce.

"If companies missed the Internet the first time around, they should be careful not to miss the wireless Web," said Ken Dulaney, an analyst at the Gartner Group in San Jose, California.

America Online, the nation's largest Internet service, announced several agreements with companies developing wireless technology that would enable customers to access the Web anytime, anyplace. "There's no question that we're on the eve of an explosion of consumers moving to wireless," said Steve Case, AOL chief executive.

Most e-commerce businesses can benefit from wireless Web technology, but this is especially true for news services, travel information sites, banks and other financial services, and book and music sellers. "For any company that has a consumer-based Web site where consumers get any kind of information, it definitely makes sense for the company to make the site wireless friendly," said Elliott Hamilton, a Web commerce analyst at the Strategis Group in Washington, DC.

Gigahertz Computer Chips

Another computer revolution began with the technology of developing ever-increasing memory and speed capabilities of computer chips. In the spring of 2000, Advanced Micro Devices (AMD) became the first semiconductor company to mass produce a personal computer microprocessor with a speed of 1 gigahertz, or 1,000 megahertz, or a billion bytes per second. That's quite a quantum leap from the IBM computer introduced in 1981 that had what they considered to be an astronomical power of 4.77 megahertz.

Shortly after AMD's achievement, the Intel Corporation followed with an announcement of its own high-speed Pentium III gigahertz chip. Computer manufacturers immediately began taking orders to install the new technology in new gigahertz PCs. The extra speed would help Web designers create more advanced interactive features, and video game developers could manipulate graphics faster and create exciting three-dimensional effects.

The Sound of Music on the Web

Other recent Web technology developments involve music. Thomas Dolby Robertson, known as Thomas Dolby during his days as a techno-rock musician in the 1980s, announced the start-up of his new company,

Beatnik Inc., which would advance the means of adding interactive sounds and music to Web sites.

Robertson expected that the "sonification" research he was promoting would go beyond the popularity of the new MP3 digital music format. By moving the cursor over various links and icons on a Web page, a variety of sounds would come up, including a company's audio jingle used in television or radio commercials. Web design training centers were starting to offer courses in Beatnik Inc.'s tools and technology, including its researchers' ideas for sonifying Web sites with sound and music.

College on the Web

The number of courses provided over the Internet at U.S. colleges and universities almost doubled between 1994 and 1998, as did enrollment in the classes. On-line courses were offered by 79 percent of four-year public colleges and 22 percent of private four-year colleges in 1998. Studying for degrees at colleges and universities by taking on-line courses appeals especially to adult students who can study via the Internet while continuing to work a regular workday.

The Web and E-Commerce

The Internet also play an increasingly important role in e-commerce. An estimated $15 billion in e-commerce was conducted via Web pages in 1999. The figure is expected to rise dramatically in the years ahead as more business is conducted electronically. An example of this was when Sears, Roebuck and Company, once a world leader in mail order purchasing through its huge paper catalog, announced in February 2000 that it was embracing e-commerce in a big new way. Company spokespersons said the retailer of everything from clothing to home repair tools was joining partners with computer software maker Oracle Corporation and Carrefour SA, a giant European retail company, to establish GlobalNetXchange.

The new venture would be the first global on-line exchange for the retail industry. Sears and Carrefour would route all their combined $80 billion in orders to suppliers who would browse the Web site and compete to fill their orders. The exchange was intended to buy and sell all kinds of retail merchandise, ranging from clothing and appliances to food. Oracle would maintain the global retail Web site, which would require the skills of hundreds or more Web designers and maintenance specialists. "This is a revolution in retail selling," said Arthur Martinez, chief executive officer of Sears. "It will cut costs for retailers, suppliers, and eventually consumers."

The Sears announcement came at about the same time that leaders of the auto industry reported they were going to become new leaders in the form of e-commerce called business-to-business or B2B commerce. B2B means businesses selling to other businesses, using the Internet to cut transaction time and costs, and to increase efficiencies in buying and selling. On-line B2B accounted for $1.76 billion in 1999 and Forrester Research predicts it will reach more than $1 trillion in 2002.

Automakers Become Web Partners

The increase of expected on-line B2B was reported in February 2000, when three of the largest automakers—General Motors, Ford, and Daimler Chrysler—announced plans to set up the world's biggest on-line marketplace for buying auto parts. It would be a giant Web site over which the automakers and their suppliers would both buy and sell the nearly $250 billion worth of auto and truck parts and other goods they buy each year—everything from engines, transmissions, brakes, and batteries to office supplies such as pens, paper, and lightbulbs.

The automakers said they hoped the business-to-business venture would cut costs and save time by streamlining their purchasing operations and putting them on-line as a cooperative buying effort. The new system would also help the automakers build more cars to customer specifications more quickly than by old-fashioned telephone ordering. The automakers' on-line cooperative would dwarf all present commercial activity on the Web. It also would be available to other automakers and their suppliers, partners, and dealers around the world and even be utilized by other industries. Again, the increased use of the Internet in commerce means more jobs for those who can design and maintain Web sites.

The Future of Web Design

The future of Web design and maintenance looks bright to Webmaster Stephen Shoaff, who says, "There will continue to be an increased demand for Web designers. Understaffing is a typical problem for Internet development in most companies. We're entering an age when the consumer will not accept dealing with a company that doesn't provide support and service through the Internet."

Michael L. Deane, former editor of *Webprofession.com*, an e-zine of the International Webmasters Association, says the future is very bright for Web designers and developers. He offers this advice to young people: "Learn HTML and new computer languages such as XHTML and XML, especially XML-Schema. Learn JavaScript. Learn Java. You don't need a college degree. Go to a technical school and get a certification in Web design. Learn one server-side scripting language such as PHP, ASP, JSP, CFML, Perl, Python, Tcl-Tk."

A career in Web design will continue to require education, experience, and keeping up with the new technology. All this can mean a lot of work, and Deane has suggestions about that: "Just have fun. Don't get into this business if having the whole world see your work will wear on your nerves. This is a pressure-packed industry. Tolerance for mediocrity will wane as the market shrinks the real on-line players down over time.

The biggest growth market for those making Web design a career is for those learning Linux, Oracle 8I, Java/Jini, and PHP/Perl skills. If you are not a graduate of Stanford University or the Massachusetts Institute of Technology or other major educational institution, then I would train in these skills to gain access to an entry-level job more easily."

Web design and development can be a very rewarding career, both financially and in job satisfaction for those who see computer technology in their future. However, Web design can also be demanding work on short deadlines requiring long and sometimes stressful hours.

Web design is always changing and will likely change greatly over the next decade and beyond, requiring continuing education and new skills in order to keep up with the increasingly sophisticated technological field, but it can also be fun.

Glossary

access To retrieve or exchange information from a computer.

browser Computer software application that permits searching for, retrieving, and viewing of content from the Web and Intranets. Well-known browsers include Netscape, Internet Explorer, and Mosaic.

chat groups Web sites that people interested in a specific topic can access for on-line discussion.

client A person or company that hires someone to do something, such as create a Web site.

consultant A person with expertise in a field who is temporarily hired by a company to perform a job on a contract basis.

data Information that can be processed by a computer.

digital A method of recording information electronically in numeric units.

document An object of a specific type as identified by the server so the client will know how to handle or display it.

e-commerce Electronic commerce. Business conducted over the Internet between purchasers and buyers.

Extranet A Web site where users can enter a secured or private area of the Internet.

fax Facsimile transmission. An electronic method of sending and receiving printed information by modem and telephone.

gopher A code that allows computer users to view text. A forerunner of the World Wide Web, it allows you to navigate up and down through means of menus to access files.

home page A Web page that serves as a starting place for a person's or organization's Web site.

HTML (hypertext markup language) Computer language used to create hypertext. It tells your browser how to display each page, which typeface or font to use, what graphics to display, and what links to create to other documents.

HTTP (hypertext transfer protocol) The system for requesting HTML documents from the hypertext links that allow users to move from one document on the Web to another.

hypertext Text with pointers (electronic links) to other text within the same document or to graphics, audio clips, or other programs.

Intranet A Web site for internal company use.

Glossary

Java A programming language making it possible to place animation and other special effects on a Web page.

multimedia The merging of text, graphics, and audio.

network A group of computers connected so they can all work together.

program The list of instructions that tell a computer how to complete a task.

script A short program written in Java, Perl, or other language that controls an aspect of a site, such as a colorful banner.

server A primary computer that stores and retrieves files for clients or Internet users.

software Computer programs that run the computer.

URL (uniform resource locator) A site's Web address. It usually starts with http://www.

Web designer or developer Someone who creates the text, graphics, and perhaps audio and video effects for a Web site.

Webmaster Someone skilled in Web design and development who oversees or is in charge of the creation of a Web site.

Web server A networked host computer that contains HTML pages served to clients via HTTP.

For More Information

In the United States

HTML Writers Guild
126 East Olympia Ave, Suite 406
Putna Gorda, FL 33950
(941) 833-0129
Web site: http://www.hwg.org

International Webmasters Association
119 E. Union Street, Suite E
Pasadena, CA 91103
(626) 449-3709
Web site: http://www.iwanet.org

World Organization of Webmasters
9580 Oak Avenue Parkway, Suite 7-177
Folsom, CA 95630
(916) 608-1597
Web site: http://www.world-webmasters.org

For More Information

In Canada

Canada Computerwork.com
http://canada.computerwork.com

Canadian Careers.com
http://www.canadiancareers.com

Career Paths Online
http://www.careerpathsonline.com/planning

Web Sites

cio.com
Web Career Research Center
http://www.cio.com/forums/careers

Computerworld
http://www.computerworld.com

eWEEK
http://www.zdnet.com/eweek

PC World
http://www.pcworld.com

Web Design Group
http://www.webdesigngroup.com

Webmaster Central
http://www.wmcentral.com

Careers in Web Design

WebmasterBase.com
http://www.webmasterbase.com

Webmasters Directory
http://webmastersdirectory.com

Webmaster Seminars
http://www.webmasterseminars.com

Webmaster Tools
http://www.mondolink.com/resource.html

Web ProForum Tutorials
http://www.iec.org/tutorials

For Further Reading

Burns, Julie Kling. *Opportunities in Computer Systems Careers.* Lincolnwood, IL: VGM Career Horizons, 1996.

Cohen, Mark H. *New Media For Kids.* New York: Market Focus Publications, 1997.

Coorough, Calleen. *Getting Started with Multimedia.* Fort Worth, TX: Dryden Press, 1998.

Davis, Jack, and Susan Merritt. *The Web Design Wow! Book.* Berkeley, CA: Peachpit Press, 1998.

Leonard, David C., and Patrick M Dillon. *Multimedia and the Web from A to Z.* Phoenix, AZ: Oryx Press, 1998.

Lund, Bill. *Getting Ready for a Career as an Internet Designer.* Mankato, MN: Capstone Press, 1998.

Careers in Web Design

Maran, Ruth. *Creating Web Pages with HTML Simplified.* Indianapolis, IN: IDG Books Worldwide, 1999.

McCanna, Laurie. *Creating Great Web Graphics.* New York: MIS Press, 1997.

McFedries, Paul. *The Complete Idiot's Guide to Creating a Web Page.* New York: Macmillan Computer Publishing, 1999.

Peck, David D. *Pocket Guide to Multimedia.* Albany, NY: Delmar Publishers, 1998.

Siegel, David. *Creating Killer Web Sites.* Indianapolis: Hayden Books, 1997.

Smith, Bud E., and Arthur Bebak. *Creating Web Pages for Dummies.* Indianapolis: IDG Books Worldwide, 1999.

Spainhour, Stephen, and Robert Eckstein. *Webmaster in a Nutshell: A Quick Desktop Reference.* Cambridge, MA: O'Reilly & Associates, 1999.

Stair, Lila B. *Careers in Computers.* Lincolnwood, IL: VGM Career Horizons, 1995.

Tracy, Joe. *Web Marketing Applied.* Cleveland, OH: Advanstar Marketing Service, 2000.

Vaughn, Joan. *Webmaster Career Starter.* New York: Learning-Express, 1999.

Index

A
Adobe Photoshop, 22, 41, 46, 47, 48, 74, 75, 92, 95
advertising, 2, 5, 20, 50, 57, 64, 109, 110, 117-118, 121
animation, 6, 10, 52, 53, 99, 109
applets, 10, 112
apprenticeships, 30

B
books on-line, 117
browsers, 3, 4, 7, 73, 77, 98, 99
business(es), 1, 2, 8, 11, 12, 14, 15, 18, 24, 25, 27, 41, 43, 44, 49-50, 57, 85, 101-102, 113, 115, 121
  starting your own, 25, 47, 48
business-to-business selling (B2B), 122-123

C
cellular phones, 118-120
college, 19-21, 25-26, 27, 28-29, 31, 36, 38, 39, 43, 48, 69, 74, 77, 80, 83, 85, 124
college courses on-line, 121
content development, 57, 70, 73, 87, 90
corporations, 3, 6, 12, 15, 27, 32, 46, 50-51, 58, 62, 69, 70, 71, 75, 78, 79, 102
cover letter, 61

D

digital technology, 116–117
Diversity in Education Initiative, 36, 38

E

e-commerce, 78, 84–86, 110, 115, 119, 121–122
editors and scripters, 97–100
education, 19–21, 61
experience, importance of, 21, 23, 24, 25, 26, 27, 29, 44, 62, 82, 100, 114, 124
extranet sites, 15, 57

F

Flash, 11, 48, 53, 108–111
frames, 10

G

gigahertz computer chips, 120
graphic design, 7, 20, 30, 40, 46, 48, 49, 52, 57, 71, 74, 75, 76, 78–79, 110
graphics, 1, 2, 3, 4, 6, 8, 10, 11, 12, 15, 21–22, 23, 42, 49, 71, 78, 79, 83, 87, 88, 89, 90, 92, 103, 105, 108, 118, 120

H

Hewlett-Packard, 30, 34, 36–39, 46, 75
high school, 2, 19, 21, 23–24, 25, 29, 39, 40–54, 60, 74

HTML, 3–4, 7, 11, 20, 32, 37, 38, 40, 42, 46, 48, 49, 64, 65, 71, 73, 74, 75, 83, 88, 90, 92, 94, 95, 97, 98, 99, 107, 109, 123
tags, 95–97
HTTP, 4
hypertext, 3, 4, 6, 11

I

interactive features, 11, 23, 37, 54, 70, 71, 84, 87, 99, 100, 109, 110, 115, 118, 120, 121
interactive video kiosks, 82–83
Internet, 1, 2, 4, 6, 7, 14, 15, 16, 18, 19, 23, 24, 25, 31, 32, 34, 35, 39, 40, 45, 50, 54, 57, 58, 66, 67, 68, 70, 72, 74, 76, 77, 78, 79, 80, 82, 83, 84, 85, 93, 94, 100, 102, 110, 111
future of, 113–124
internships, 15, 24–30, 35–39, 40, 44, 48, 74
criteria to evaluate, 27–30
Technical Teen, 31–33
interviewing, 61
intranet, 15, 57–58, 69–71, 75, 77, 78, 83, 85

Index

J
Java/JavaScript, 11, 20, 32, 37, 38, 40, 75, 83, 88, 95, 99-100, 107, 108-112

freelancing/self-employed, 3, 13, 14-15, 16, 44, 49, 56, 59-60, 65, 66, 72, 75
part-time, 74, 80
salaried for a company, 13-14, 16, 56, 57, 58, 59-60, 65, 66
working for Web development company, 3, 14, 56, 58, 69, 70
your first, 16, 60-61, 64-65
job listings on Internet, 17, 61, 72, 73, 76

L
layout, consistency of, 102, 103
links, 4, 6, 10, 22, 24, 42, 50, 51, 52, 54, 87, 89-90, 103, 104, 106, 121

M
marketing, 12, 18, 20, 50, 56, 57, 64, 67, 85, 102, 106, 108, 109, 110
mentoring, 25, 28, 34, 35, 36, 42, 45
telementoring, 34-35, 37
multimedia, 6, 40, 44, 53, 82, 114
multimedia developer, 82-83

music on the Web, 120-121

N
navigation, making it easy, 103-104
networking with people, 12, 24, 61
networks, computer, 31, 32, 38, 57, 80

O
organizations, 13, 14, 28, 30, 45, 46, 66, 101

P
photographs, 21, 50, 52, 89, 90, 92, 108, 110, 112
placement agencies, 78-79
planning a Web site, 101-102
Plugged-In Enterprises, 45-48
portfolio, 24, 43, 48, 75
programming, 2, 7, 20, 32, 42, 47, 57, 64, 70, 76, 82, 87, 88, 95, 107, 108, 109, 111

R
registering a Web site, 92-94, 106
résumé, 25, 36, 60-62, 73, 75, 76
sample, 63
reverse-engineering, 74

S

scanning, 6, 44, 74, 92
scholarships, 36, 38
school-to-work programs, 25, 41, 43, 45
scripters, 99-100
selling products, 2, 3, 4, 18, 57, 58, 66, 67, 68, 72, 83, 84, 101, 121-123
servers, 3, 4, 7, 42, 93
software, 1, 3, 7, 18, 22, 23, 31, 41, 57, 77, 78, 80, 81, 83, 88, 90, 95, 99, 101, 118
sound/audio, 3, 4, 6, 10, 18, 23, 52, 82, 83, 87, 116, 118, 121
speed of Web sites, 66-68, 84, 86, 99, 106, 120
systems engineer, 80-81

T

team (of specialists), 7, 8, 12, 18, 31, 41, 42, 47, 57, 65, 76, 80, 83, 87, 102, 112, 114, 115
technical/trade schools, 19, 20, 21, 60, 124
technical support representative, 79-80
testing your Web site, 93, 100

text, 2, 3, 4, 6, 10, 23, 42, 49, 50, 52, 76, 87, 88, 89, 90, 92, 114, 118
text editors, 97-98

U

uploading a site, 93
URL, 93

V

video, 52, 82, 83, 87, 116, 120
voice mail, 117-118

W

Web consultant, 81-82
Web design, 2, 3, 10, 11-13, 16-18, 19-24, 26, 28, 30, 34, 35, 36, 39, 43, 44, 46, 47, 53, 54, 56, 57, 58, 61, 64-67, 69, 72, 74-76, 77, 81, 87-92, 94, 97, 103, 107-112, 114
   future of, 113-124
   help regarding, 23, 94-95
   history of, 7-8
   mistakes to avoid, 105-107
   related careers, 76-86
   tips on, 100-105
Web development, 2, 3, 7, 10, 11-13, 32, 39, 44, 57, 58, 59, 60, 65, 69, 70, 71, 72, 76, 77, 78, 80, 84, 85, 87-92, 107, 108-112, 114

Index

Web domain names, 116
Web, history of, 5-8
Web marketing, 83, 109
Webmasters, 7, 8, 12, 16, 18, 19, 30, 35, 57, 67, 70, 71, 75, 76-77, 93, 94, 101, 115, 123
Webmaster School, 35, 40-45
Web pages, 1, 4, 8, 10, 12, 18, 19, 20, 21, 22-24, 32, 38, 44, 47, 65, 71, 76, 83, 101, 116
    types of, 49-54
    what is on them, 87-88
Web sites, creating, 2, 10, 12, 18, 64, 87-92, 114
    debate on skills required, 107-112
Web sites for non-profits, 42, 72-73
Web sites, maintaining/updating, 10, 15, 18, 57, 58, 65, 69, 70, 80, 82, 102, 114, 117, 123
wireless Web, 118-120
women, opportunities for, 18, 38
workplaces, casual, 59, 79
writing, 8, 12, 21, 41, 57, 75, 87, 88

Photo Credits

Cover by Kristen Artz; p.11 © VCG/FPG; pp.16, 33, 60, 67, 91, 106 and 114 by Kristen Artz; p.22 and 78 by Sam Jordan

Series Design and Layout

Danielle Goldblatt